THE COMPLETE
PUG

Three Pugs. By Walter Harrowing (1882).

Ellen S. Brown

Howell Book House

HOWELL
BOOK
HOUSE

New York

HOWELL BOOK HOUSE
A Simon & Schuster / Macmillan Company
1633 Broadway
New York, NY 10019

MACMILLAN is a registered trademark of Macmillan, Inc.

Library of Congress Cataloging-in-Publication data
available on request.

ISBN 0–87605–263-4

Manufactured in Singapore

10 9 8 7 6 5 4 3 2 1

CONTENTS

I dedicate this book to
my late husband
ARTHUR BROWN
with whom I spent 50 happy years.
For 30 years we enjoyed the company of
our beloved Pugs
and the pleasure of the show ring.

Goodchance Camellia and Goodchance Little Rosa.

Photo: John Hartley

ACKNOWLEDGEMENTS

I felt greatly honoured when asked to write this book. As the Pug Dog Club Historian for the past twelve years, I have learned so much about the Pug that it was delightful to get it down on paper. I hope readers will enjoy reading it as much as I have enjoyed writing it.

My grateful thanks must first go to my daughter, Yvonne Naylor: I have kept her so busy typing for me. I could not have done this book without her help.

Thanks also to Sophie Mount for her sketches. To the many members who helped in obtaining pictures and photographs and to all my friends overseas who supplied me with such valuable information about their own countries, I am indeed grateful. Thank you to Marion Adair, Robert Carlough, and Edward and Charlotte Patterson (America), Ray Alexandra, Patsy Muirden and Bonny Richardson (Australia), Ingrid Mylemans (Belgium), Moira Grant-Cooke (Eire), Carolien van Deimen (Holland), Lundi Blamey and Jack Hulley (South Africa) and Marianne Ekedahl (Sweden).

E.S.B. 1997

6

*I*NTRODUCTION: GETTING TO KNOW THE PUG

The Pug is a small dog, yet sturdy, strong. Happy and always contented, not in the least temperamental, the Pug is one of the most delightful breeds anyone could wish to own. This friendly little dog loves people, especially children, who, in return, love and enjoy a Pug's company. The Pug is dignified, with a lovely character, is inquisitive and curious but not intrusive, enjoys all the petting and pampering you can give and has plenty of intelligence. It is often said that a Pug is a perfect partner for the elderly. Maybe so, for there is nothing Pugs like better than sharing their owner's armchair. Certainly a Pug loves comfort.

The Pug is square, compact and cobby, weighing between 14 and 18 pounds (6.4 to 8.2 kg) so is easy to keep as, being small, the dog needs little exercise. Providing your Pug has a daily walk, or if you have a good size garden that can be used freely, the dog is truly contented. That does not mean a Pug does not enjoy a romp, for Pugs have plenty of energy for outdoor life. Most Pugs will eat and enjoy their food and usually ask for more. This has to be watched so as to avoid the dog becoming too heavy. The Pug is easy to groom. The short coat needs just a brush every day and the occasional bath. Ears must be kept clean and a careful watch maintained on the eyes and nose wrinkle.

The Pug makes a very satisfactory house dog and will bark for the door bell and telephone, which one finds most beneficial. These little dogs are good mixers with other dogs and are quite brave with larger breeds. Somehow the Pug always seems to attract attention in public, more than any other breed of dog. I am sure this dates back to their aristocratic breeding. They will hold themselves aloof and look at people with those lovely, large, dark eyes as if to say: "Look me over, I'm very important". Moreover, to every owner, their Pug is the most important member of the family and demands indulgence.

Of course the Pug may seem different in appearance and may be funny just to look at, especially to those not familiar with the breed. Part of a Pug's charm lies in this strange structure.

Somehow the Pug seems different, like no other breed. We owners say: "There are dogs and there are Pugs". They have that special something. Having a Pug as a companion one becomes besotted for ever

One of the most distinctive looking of all dogs, the Pug is an ideal companion.

Photos: Carol Ann Johnson.

and that has proved itself through history to the present day. Once you own a Pug, that will be your breed for life and it seems to carry on through families.

However, if you have never had anything to do with this breed of dog, their appearance may take some getting used to. As is often said: "You either adore them or dislike them". Admittedly they have no glamour, but beauty is only in the eye of the beholder.

Pugs have personality plus and this is what wins their way into so many hearts. Above all they love their owners and are not afraid to show it. So, what happens? You return that love two-fold. It is said that they snore and grunt. Not all Pugs snore. One, now and again, might, but that applies to all breeds. So, in this respect, do not think of them as different from any

other dog. I suppose they do grunt at times but I think this is when they are trying to say something to you. Yes, a Pug is very human in many ways and will try to get the last word in. Some Pugs snort. If that happens a lot then there could be a little weakness with the soft palate, but this is nothing to worry about unduly, unless it is really troublesome.

I have often been asked: "Why did you choose a Pug?" I never chose a Pug – fate brought us together when, one evening in 1963, my telephone rang. The caller informed me that he knew of a twelve-week-old puppy in need of a good home. "I thought of you because I know you have just lost your last Cocker Spaniel," he said. (I bred these for fifteen years.) "No," I said. "I don't think I am interested." Later that evening the caller visited me. "I've

come to explain about the puppy. It is in a good home but the owner suffers from multiple sclerosis and fell over the puppy. On doctor's orders puppy must go." How could I resist this story? I had no idea what breed this puppy was until, going out of the door to collect him for me, my visitor said, "By the way, it's a Pug. Do you know what a Pug is?" "Yes," said I, "a small, flat-nosed dog."

Sonee came to me one hour later and the memory is as clear to me as if it was yesterday. I fell for him immediately and spent the rest of that week repeating, "I am glad I've got you, I am glad I've got you." He was such a joy, such a character. I was overwhelmed. My love and enthusiasm for the breed just grew and grew. My Sonee soon had a black companion, Satchmo. Then came another black, Rory. Three years later I decided I would like to breed, so my three boys had a fawn lady companion, Wilhelmina. I had become infatuated with this captivating breed.

DISTINGUISHED PUG OWNERS

In many families the Pug dog is a must. Time and time again one meets people who say, "We have always had a Pug in our family," and this appears to go through to generations. The late Duke and Duchess of Windsor were great lovers of the Pug. Many of them were from American breeding, although at least three of them were bred in England. These were Masberk Disraeli (bred by Miss Masland), Goldengleam Trouper (bred by Wendy Allen) and Normpug Black Minora (bred by Mrs Washington-Hibbert). The late Duchess of Windsor visited The Pug Dog Club Championship Show in 1965. She was looking to buy another black Pug. She would have made a good judge because she certainly knew what points of a Pug to look for.

In Charlene Bry's book *The Truth about the Duchess* we learn how well her pet Pugs lived. They were sprayed daily with Christian Dior perfume and dressed in mink collars. They ate fresh capon breast, steak or liver served with freshly-baked biscuits on silver dishes. The Duchess of Windsor once remarked: "My Pugs took the place of the children I never had." The Duke was very fond of his Pugs and his end was very sad. His Pug dog Diamond always slept on his bed. Twelve days before the Duke died Diamond stayed out of the room and the Duke constantly asked for him but would not let anyone bring the Pug in. The Duke would say: "He'll come back when he wants to." On the Friday

Introduction

after the Duchess had said "Goodnight" to the Duke, there was a persistent scratching on the door. Diamond had come back. "Diamond," the Duke's nurse heard the Duke say, "You are a most faithful friend." He slept that night his hand on the Pug's head. Throughout Saturday, the last day of his life, both Diamond and the Duchess were with him.

It was reported in the newspaper on August 15th 1972 that "James, the Duke of Windsor's favourite Pug dog, pined after his master's death in May. He would go to the Duke's bedroom in his Paris home every morning, scratching on the door for a breakfast biscuit. After weeks of slinking away under the Duke's favourite armchair,

James refused all food. A vet was called but there was little he could do for the pining Pug and now James has died of a broken heart." Jean Manifold had the privilege of visiting the home-in-exile of the late Duke and Duchess, a mansion in the Bois de Boulogne, now completely restored and owned by Mohammed Al Fayed. (Al Fayed is also the owner of Harrods in Kensington, London.) Jean was overwhelmed at the love and devotion that the Duke and Duchess had for their Pugs. In every room there were ornaments and pictures and reminiscences of them. Talking to Monsieur Martin, the Duke's senior servant, she heard many stories of their beloved pets. When mention is made of the

The Duke and Duchess of Windsor with two of their Pugs at a dog show in France in the late 1950s.   *Photo courtesy of the Al Fayed Archives.*

Duke's favourite Pug who was with him until the end in 1972, names do get a little confusing in the newspaper articles. Monsieur Martin says it was Minaroo, elsewhere I have read Diamond and when his Pug died it was named as James. Maybe they were different Pugs, for the Windsors did have many.

Quite recently an article was written in a weekly journal about Lord and Lady Christie. The Christie family have lived at Glyndebourne in Sussex since 1860 and four generations of them have shared the same passion for Pug dogs. Sir George Christie says he can hardly remember a time when there was not a Pug in the house. He feels that if the Pugs left, their Glyndebourne Opera House would close – just as the royal family would fall if the ravens left the Tower of London. Outside the new theatre stands a bust of Sir George's father supported by two Pugs. In 1985 Sir George and Lady Christie opened the grounds of Glyndebourne for the Pug Dog Club's annual garden party. The weather was perfect and over 150 guests were present, all with their Pugs. There were games, competitions, a raffle and plenty to eat. It was a most enjoyable and memorable day.

Lady Montagu Douglas Scott, the horticulturist Valerie Finnis, became a Pug devotee when one saved her mother's life by jumping on her sick bed and snapping her out of unconsciousness. When she lost her beloved Pug, Sophie, she had a memorial erected with the inscription "Canis erat sed amica vera" (She was a dog, but a true friend). We all understand those heartaches. What was it Kipling wrote? "Brothers and sisters, I bid you beware of giving your heart for a dog to tear."

Lady Braye is always eager to talk about

Lady George Christie with Pug, Phoebe, at Glyndebourne, Sussex.

her black Pug, Tang, and her association with Pugs. Lady Robinson tells how her family have had Pugs for generations and her husband Sir John Robinson grew up with Pugs in Kenya. He had as a neighbour there, Lady Delamere. I know Lady Delamere owned Pugs for I remember meeting her when she was on a visit to England in 1971. Her Ladyship took back home with her Harvest of Greentubs, whom she had obtained from Mrs Cooke. The Hon. Sarah Lawson Johnstone told me herself, quite recently, how Pugs have been

in her family for many generations. These three honourable ladies, Braye, Robinson and Johnstone, meet each year for their Pugs' Tea party, keeping up the tradition, I'm sure, of the famous Pugs' Tea Party in 1850 which was given by the Rev William Davenport-Bromley in Baginton, Warwickshire.

Sir Winston Churchill also owned a Pug when his children were young. His Pug became the special pet of his daughter Mary. At one point 'Pug' became desperately ill. Mary was in tears. Churchill was greatly upset at her distress and although he really thought that poetry, though enjoyable, was a minor sort of thing, prose being very much more important, he composed this ditty for Mary:

"Oh what is the matter with poor Puggy-Wug,
Pet him and kiss him and give him a hug,
Run and fetch him a suitable drug,
Wrap him up tenderly all in a rug,
That is the way to cure Puggy-Wug."

In 1974, the year of the centenary of the birth of Sir Winston Churchill, the BBC made a film called *Walk with Destiny*, based on Sir Winston's history of Word War II, *The Gathering Storm* . The BBC required a Pug to include in the film and my own Goodchance My Delila took the part. Richard Burton who was the chosen actor to take the part of Sir Winston Churchill really fell for Delila and offered me a large sum of money for her, but I would not part with her. This became big news when the headline in one Sunday paper read: "A Brush Off For Burton from Delila the Starlet".

Randolph Churchill, Sir Winston's son, owned a family of black Pugs. I have also seen pictures of David Hicks, son-in-law of

ABOVE: Gilbert Harding, the famous TV personality of the late 1950s, with his Pug.

LEFT Zena Dare, the famous actress at the end of the 19th Century.

the late Lord Mountbatten, with his Pugs. Donald McCleary, the well-known ballet dancer and master, has owned Pugs for many years and they have been most familiar with members of The Royal Opera House, Covent Garden. Lou Freston has three Pugs who used to accompany her every day to the Houses of Parliament where she works. There was also a black Pug who walked the grounds of the Tower of London. He was owned by one of the Beefeaters. Valentino, the famous Italian Top Couturier, has many Pugs. Valentina Tereshkova, the Russian cosmonaut, became the first woman in space and it was a Pug she chose as her pet. A book was released in 1993, thirty years after her wonderful adventure, where she said: "As I saw the planet from space I realised how small Earth is and how fragile. Lands and oceans have no nationalities, they are not Russian or British, they are planetary." On the back of the sleeve of the book is a most delightful photograph of Valentina with her pet Pug. This is a picture that I know she treasures.

Some years ago I was talking to Countess Bismarck who told me that when Queen Victoria died a number of her Pugs were taken back to Germany by Princess Victoria, the Queen's eldest daughter, who was married to Prince Frederick, who became the German Emperor. Count Bismarck, a great friend of the Princess and her husband, was given one of these Pugs. The Countess told me that the Count, who was her great-grandfather, said "From that day on Pugs should always be in the family." "We keep and breed from our own stock," said the Countess, "but occasionally

ABOVE: Goodchance My Delila with Richard Burton in the TV Film "Walk with Destiny", December, 1974.

RIGHT: Gretchen Franklin as 'Ethel' with 'Willie' in Eastenders, BBC TV.

we like to introduce fresh blood." How sensible!

The Pug Dog Willie made quite a name for himself when he appeared as the companion of Gretchen Franklin in the BBC soap *Eastenders*. Willie was owned by Jan Rouke who ran an animal agency. In a letter which I received from her at that time she said, "We are really delighted with William, quite apart from the fact that he is a very good working dog, he is the most incredibly nice person. He loves all people and all other dogs and is such a lovely character as well as a personality. He has given us hours of fun and laughter." Gretchen Franklin told me herself that she would have loved to have had Willie as her own, but Jan would not part with him.

W.L. Lloyd-Jones was well known for his Dene's Veterinary Medical products. Throughout his life Buster, as he was known to his friends, suffered from polio which eventually confined him to a wheelchair. He was known to thousands of animal lovers as probably the most skilful vet ever to have practised his art. When Buster, because of his disability, had to give up Denes Close, the house he loved so much and where he had kept so many animals, he couldn't bear to be without animals around him, so he bought a Pug puppy and called him Puddy. Buster said, "He finds it perfectly natural that I should move on wheels and not on legs and a dear friend he has been to me from the start." His autobiography is interesting reading.

Going back in time, Harriet Beecher Stowe, the American author of *Uncle Tom's Cabin*, published in 1852, was a Pug fancier who owned two Pugs named Punch and Missy. More recently Gilbert Harding, Sir Ralph Richardson, Cecil Beaton, Sammy Davis Jr., Paul Winfield and Anton Walbrook are all known to have owned Pugs. Certainly the Pug is an aristocratic breed that lived and still lives with a host of celebrities from all walks of life.

1 THE HISTORY OF THE PUG

The true origin of the Pug has never really been traced, despite all the research that has gone on through the years to find where the Pug came from. In my opinion there is no doubt whatsoever that the Pug originated in the East, from China. I know that many people have come to the same conclusion and have the same view. Throughout the known history of China, the people of that vast country have respected the dog, breeding and keeping them for hunting, food, pelts and leather, as well as for companionship. Perhaps it could be that the 'Chancien' or dog-feeder was the first dog judge, as in 1115 BC his job was to judge the quality and character of different dogs from their appearance. But we are not sure for what purpose he was judging them.

A small 'short-mouthed' dog can be traced back to Confucius (b. 551 BC) but it is believed that these were sporting dogs, not toy dogs. Many of the records of the history of China were destroyed by Emperor Ch'in Shih (225 BC) so there is a big gap in information available. The first clear reference appears to be in AD 732 when a 'Ssuchuan pai dog' was among the tributes sent from a Korean State to Japan.

'Pai' indicated a short-faced dog with short legs. These dogs were said to have been small enough to go under the very low tables around which the Chinese sat on mats. In the province of Ssuchuan was an important town called Lo-Chiang and hence, from about AD 950 onwards, the Ssuchuan pai dog was referred to as the 'Lo-Chiang-sze' or 'Lo-Chiang'. At a later date it became 'Lo-sze', which in the early days of the 19th century was the Chinese name for Pug. Lo-sze were extremely popular in China from AD 969 to AD 1153 during the Sung Dynasty, but during the fourteenth and fifteenth centuries, at the time of the Ming Dynasty, they were ousted from popularity by the cat. There still exist some Imperial dog books dating back to the late seventeenth century in which there are detailed illustrations of all the breeds of dog in China. In one of these books (date unknown) there is a picture of a dog which has a strong resemblance to a Pug.

As the exact translation of documents from China is difficult, we have to look at drawings and scrolls to observe the appearance of the Chinese dogs. From these it seems that, at this time, there were

Early Pug models from the reign of Ch'ien Lung 1736-95, on show at Saltram House, Plympton, Devon.

three main types of dog in China – the Lo-sze, the Pekingese and the Lion Dog. It has often been said that these dogs could have been Pugs, Pekingese and Japanese Spaniels. The important characteristics of the Lo-sze were the shortness of coat and the elasticity of skin, both of which are far greater in the Pug than in the Pekingese. Also, the point most sought after by the Chinese breeders was the 'Prince Mark', formed by wrinkles on the forehead, with a vertical bar, in imitation of the Chinese character for 'Prince'. The button or-white blaze on the forehead was also encouraged in the Lo-sze, but not as much as the wrinkles. The flat face, square jaw and small ears were also known; so was the curly tail. I feel sure that the 'Lo-sze' must have been the forefather of our present-day Pug. Some ancient pictures of Chinese Lo-sze show them wearing collars with bells, a fashion that was adopted in Europe many centuries later.

Much as I would like to, I cannot avoid mentioning the alternative suggestions about the origin of the Pug. One idea is that many years ago the short face of the Pug was achieved by crushing or damaging the nasal bones while the dog was a puppy. How absurd! This would not result in the descendants having short faces and I cannot take this suggestion seriously. In the 1950s George Featherstone of Tunbridge Wells conducted a great deal of original research at the British Museum into the history and origin of the Pug. As a result it was his opinion that "the exact origin of the Pug is a matter of conjecture and although modern writers attribute this to China, there seems to be little or no evidence to warrant this statement", and we must give him credit for all his hard work. Some may say that if you look at old pictures of Pugs, such as the beautiful drawing by Reinagle (1805), they look like small Mastiffs or Bulldogs. To try to substantiate this line of thinking, study has been made of the skull of a pure-bred Pug. The result was that it has been found that certain details of its structure are different from breeds such as the Bulldog and other short-faced Bull breeds. These details are only present in the Oriental short-faced Toy dogs. So this is another suggestion as to the origin of the Pug that I cannot accept.

During the late 1950s there were many articles written in the Pug Dog Club's *Bulletin* concerning the conflicting opinions held by George Featherstone and Wilhelmine Swainston-Goodger – the former claiming that Pugs are scaled-down versions of the Mastiff and the latter believing that Pugs originated in China. I must say that I do not agree with the ideas of George Featherstone, but am strongly in favour of the school of thought that the Pug did originate in China. But how did Pugs arrive in Europe?

HOLLAND

After those early descriptions, very little was written about these dogs until 1572, when we have a clear reference to the Pug. It appears that when the Spanish made a surprise attack on the Dutch camp at Hermigny on September 11th 1572, a Pug saved the life of William the Silent. In his *Actions of the Lowe Countries* (1618) Sir Roger Williams wrote: "For I heard the Prince say often, that as hee thought, but for a dog he had been taken. The Camisado was given with such resolution, that the place of armes took no alarme, untill these fellowes were running in with the enemies in their tailes. Whereupon the dogge, hearing a great noyse, fell to scratching and crying and withall leapt on the Prince's face, awaking him being asleep, before any of his men. And albeit the Prince lay in his armes, with a lackey alwaies holding one of his horses ready bridled: yet at the going

out of his tent, with much adoe he recovered his horse before the enemie arrived. Nevertheless one of his Quiries was slaine taking horse presently after him: and divers of his servants were forced to escape amongst the guards of foote, which could not recover their horses. For the truth ever since, untill the Prince's dying day, he kept one of that dog's race: so did many of his friendes and followers. The most of all of these dogs were white little houndes, with crooked noses, called camuses." ('Camus' is a French word meaning 'snub-nosed'.) This little dog's name was probably Pompey, and the Prince was always grateful to him for saving his life. So here we have a classic story in the history of the Pug, as well as a significant episode which is said to have influenced the history of Europe.

The Pugs, with their orange-coloured ribbons, were great favourites of the Dutch Royal family, so much so that when William and Mary of Orange came to England to be King and Queen in 1688, they brought along with them their lovely and adored Pugs, complete with orange ribbons. Soon the aristocracy in England fell for the breed and the Pug became immensely popular.

Now, how did the Pug arrive in Europe? There can be but one answer. The European trade with China, after an absence of some centuries, was resumed between Canton in the East and Portugal in the West in 1516. Trade with Spain, Holland and England followed shortly afterwards, and there is no doubt that a number of these small dogs arrived in Spain with the cargo and made their way to other parts of Europe. By the seventeenth century the Pug was very much favoured. The painting of The Marquesa de Pontejos (1785) by Francisco José de Goya shows clearly what lovely Pugs were being bred in Spain at this time.

RUSSIA

Just how long Pugs have been in Russia is hard to say. The Princess Provost Hedwig Sophie Augusta, maiden aunt of Catherine the Great of Russia (1729-1796), was a great lover of dogs and especially Pugs. It is said that at one time she kept as many as sixteen in her chamber. A maid was employed to keep them clean, which took a whole day to attend to. When the Princess drove out she always had many of her Pugs with her and they even accompanied her to church. She seemed to spend all her days besotted by her Pugs, who commanded all her attention, somewhat to the detriment of her education and her appearance. Many books published between 1800 and 1860 have mentioned the Pug dog in Germany, France, Austria, Spain and Moscow, so by then the breed had become quite widespread.

GERMANY

In Germany during early days the breed was called 'Mopshond', derived from a Dutch word, 'Mopperan', meaning to mope or to look peevish. Later it became 'Mopshund' and finally 'Mops', the name that is used today. The popularity of Mops in Germany in the first half of the eighteenth century is clearly shown by the numerous Pug models created at the Meissen factory in Saxony. It is said that these models were designed from life studies, the Pugs being owned by the managers of the factory. It was during the 1700s that the idea of having the Pug's ears cropped was introduced, which is so clearly shown in the Meissen models. These porcelain figures are in great demand at the present time. The Pug played an important part in Saxony in 1736, for it was then that the Pope excommunicated the Masons in

Germany. The Elector of Saxony, who was the most important patron of Meissen, was also Grand Master of the Freemasons. In order to continue operating, the Masons did so in an underground way, concealing their identity by calling themselves 'Mopsorden' or 'The Order of the Pug'. The Pug was their secret symbol.

FRANCE

France took the name of 'Carlin' for the Pug, from a French actor by the name of Carlin who, in the early eighteenth century, performed as a Harlequin, wearing a black mask resembling that of the Pug. The most famous Pug in the history of France must be Fortuné. He was said to be no beauty, for he was russet in colour and had a long body and short legs, but he did have the characteristic black muzzle and curly tail of a Pug. Being the much loved pet of Empress Josephine, he apparently was not particularly fond of Napoleon Buonaparte. Napoleon told a friend that he found Fortuné in possession of Josephine's bed on his wedding night and that he, not liking an intruder, took a piece out of Napoleon's leg. But Napoleon bore no malice and grew to love the little Pug. When Fortuné died, after a disagreement with the cook's Bulldog, Josephine was so distressed that a successor was soon obtained for her and for the rest of her life she possessed a Pug.

ENGLAND

There is little evidence of there being Pugs in England before they arrived with William and Mary of Orange in this country in 1688. However, the 18th century brought the Pug very much to the fore. The renowned English painter, William Hogarth, was exceptionally fond of his Pug

TOP LEFT: Pug Dog published August 1798.
ABOVE: Pug Dogs by Reinagle from Taplin's
"Sportsmans Cabinet" 1803.
LEFT: Wood carving of "Punch and Tetty", Pugs
the property of Mr C. Morrison of Walham
Green, mid 19th century.

called Trump and included him in his famous self-portrait. Trump was just one of the Pugs that he owned and his love of the breed was very obvious.

But, what of the name, *Pug*? That question has many answers. The word 'Pug', 'Pugg' and 'Pugge' was used as a term of endearment, as meaning mischievous or impish, or to mean a small pet monkey. Bailey wrote in his dictionary in 1731: "Pug – a Nickname for a Monkey or Dog." Although there were other meanings, this definition of 'Pug' stayed,

An early prize-winning Pug, 1907, without doubt a Willoughby breeding.

24 years later, in the dictionary of Samuel Johnson (1755). One Victorian writer, the Rev. T. Pearce, whose pseudonym was 'Idstone', suggested that it derived from the Latin word 'Pugnus' (a fist) because the profile of the dog's head seemed to resemble a clenched fist. However, whatever the reason, the name has remained as Pug, the shortest name of any breed of dog.

By the mid-nineteenth century certain names of breeders were becoming quite well-known. Lord and Lady Willoughby d'Eresby, from Grimsthorpe near Lincoln, were such breeders. The Willoughby Pugs have been said to have come from Russia, imported from St Petersburg, and were obtained from 'the female Blondin', a lady tight-rope walker. Others say these Pugs were obtained from Vienna, having been purchased from a Hungarian countess. However it was known that Lord and Lady Willoughby were trying to improve their stock by introducing foreign strains, so they could have obtained them from both. The Willoughby Pugs were of a darker colour,

Another early Pug of about the same time. This surely is a Morrison breeding.

sometimes called 'pepper and salt', because of the mixture of fawn and black hair.

At the same period of time, a Mr Charlie Morrison, a publican from Walham Green in London, was in possession of the richer and more yellow fawn-coloured Pug. The Morrison Pugs were pure-bred from Dutch bloodlines, present in the Royal kennels of Queen Charlotte, wife of George III. The story goes that they came from the Royal household through the back door. (Some workings of the waiter, the butler and the upstairs maid, I should think!) Still, no matter when and how they were obtained, these Pugs and the Willoughbys' are the forefathers of our present-day Pugs. By 1870, Lord and Lady Willoughby and Charlie Morrison had decided that the time had come at last to use each other's stock, as the demand for the Pug was reaching a peak. There is no longer a pure unmixed specimen of either strain, but the two types assert themselves in today's Pugs and can be traced to their respective origins. The Pug Dog Club of England, which had been unofficially formed in 1881, was accepted

on the English KC register in 1883. Champion Pugs have been registered at the KC since 1886.

AMERICA

The Pug was accepted by the American Kennel Club in 1885. According to Filomena Doherty (*Pet Pug* 1961), there was only one registration, but I have found no other reference regarding this Pug. It is interesting to compare this with the first volume of the English Kennel Club Stud

"Some Puggie Expressions"
An illustration from The Strand
Magazine (1892). The artist is unknown
but is thought to be Louis Wain.

Book (1874) where almost ten years earlier sixty-six Pugs were registered. Pugs were beginning to be imported into America from England as far back as 1897. It was reported in the *Ladies' Kennel Journal* in October of that year that Mrs Selfridge bought three beautiful black puppies from Mrs Trested Clarke and took them with her to America. The *Ladies' Kennel Journal* also reported in 1900 that Black Night was sold to Mrs Howard Gould of New York for £200 and Canonbury Princess was sold to the same lady for £150. These were both high prices for the day.

At the turn of the century it is recorded that Al G. Eberhardt of Camp Dennison, Ohio was the foremost breeder of the Pug in America. Would this be the gentleman from the Rookery Kennels in Painsville, Ohio, said to own 'the strongest kennel of sires in America'? In 1897 he was importing a number of Pugs from England, the Finsbury Pugs, which were bred by Miss L.E. Harris, and the Haughty Pugs, bred by Mrs C. Houlker. It is interesting to note that one of Mrs Houlker's famous Pugs, Eng. Ch. Haughty Madge, was one of the first Pugs to be registered in America. Both Miss Harris and Mrs Houlker were breeding and successfully showing Pugs in England from 1888 through to the beginning of this century.

A lady said to have had Pugs in America at the turn of the century was Mrs L.C. Smith of Long Beach, California. She used Cupid as her prefix but I cannot trace any of her breeding. Dr M.H. Cryer is another gentleman who was an early pioneer of the Pug, with imports from England. Since some of these imports went back to Click, son of Lamb and Moss (mentioned later in this book), he must have been importing in the late 1800s.

By 1928 more Pugs were being imported to America from England. Mrs Sarah Given Waller was one very enthusiastic lady at that time eager to popularise the Pug Dog. She was said to have had about one hundred Pugs in her Sigvale Kennels. She very much favoured the Broadway Pugs, bred by Mrs E.N. Power in England, a lady after her own heart, for her Broadway Kennels were the largest in England and, it has been said, probably in the world. However, these ladies, so many miles apart, must have seen eye to eye, because Mrs Waller imported many Broadway Pugs into America. I am sure Mrs Power must have sold her the best of her stock, for there were quite a number of Broadway Champions among the early stock of Mrs Waller. Mrs Power's Pugs were of good quality and were shown very successfully in England. It was at this time that black Pugs began to make their presence felt. They were steadily increasing in number at the Shows and beginning to take awards.

THE BLACK PUG

Lady Brassey, who was famous for her voyages to the far East and writing journals on her experiences, was quite happy to take her Pugs on her voyages with her. On January 19th 1882 she wrote in her diary: "Somewhat to our surprise, we this morning found that an unexpected addition to our family of dogs had taken place during the night. Nigger, my little black pug, had given birth to a puppy. It was a great beauty but sad to say it only survived a few hours. By an unfortunate accident the cage containing all the dogs was carried up on deck in the cold morning fog, and the poor little puppy no doubt perished in consequence. Poor little Nigger seems very well, notwithstanding the loss of her only child. I am so sorry for its death! It was such a beauty!"

On January 20th 1882, Lady Brassey wrote: "Poor Nigger was very ill all day, getting worse towards the evening, in spite of all we could do for her, which was not much. The last twenty-four hours of the faithful creature's life were inexpressibly painful to me, as her pleading painful eyes looked to me for help and relief from pain I could not give. She took every remedy with loving confidence from my hand, as if she understood it was to do her good. After lingering in what I fear was great pain, though she never uttered a cry, she died in the night in my lap, or rather at half past two on Saturday morning. And so ended the life of one of the dearest little dogs that ever breathed, to the regret of everyone on board; for though devoted to me, she was a favourite with all. All admiring her little winning ways and engaging manners, and there were few dry eyes among the crew or servants when they heard of her death."

Lady Brassey was devoted to her black Pugs and, as one finds from reading through her diaries, she had many of them, bred mostly from her own stock. Yet no-one ever asked her how she came by them originally.   In 1886 a show held at Maidstone in Kent had a number of black Pugs entered by Lady Brassey. She had a black class all to herself. The result was: 1st Jacopo; 2nd Nap; 3rd Jack Spratt; 4th Bessie Spratt. It is understood that these black Pugs were brought back to England from China by Lady Brassey on her return from one of her Far East voyages. It has also been said that these were the first black Pugs in England, but this can be disproved. Hogarth's painting *The House of Cards* (1730) clearly shows a black Pug, and Queen Victoria is said to have owned one

before the Maidstone Show in 1886 and, according to these records, so did Lady Brassey. But, one must admit, it was Lady Brassey who started the fashion for the black Pug and certainly she was the first to exhibit one.

THE VICTORIAN ERA

By now we have reached the Victorian age and this surely was the ultimate for Pug popularity, especially among the aristocracy. They were seen, loved and pampered by one and all who could afford them. There was no doubt it was the genteel ladies who owned them, so they must have fetched a good price. Reading through a fashion album recently I came across the following: "The cult of being seen with ornamental animals persisted throughout the eighteenth and nineteenth centuries. Lap dogs were the perfect accessories of indolence since they required no exercise. Thus Lady Bertram in Jane Austen's *Mansfield Park* spent her days sitting, nicely dressed, on a sofa doing some long piece of needlework of little use and beauty, thinking more of her Pug than her children."

After a bill for women's votes had been defeated in 1870, *Punch* asked "What else could one expect, for:-

"Would you then know my Celia's charms,
She carries Pug dogs in her arms,
E'er dresses in the newest taste,
By lacing tight deforms her waist..."

Towards the end of Edward VII's reign *Punch* declared: "The cult of the toy dog has reached a stage when ladies have to look at the little darlings through a microscope." The 'little darlings' were Pomeranians and miniature Pug dogs decked out in ribbons matching those of

TOP LEFT: *Queen Victoria's Pugs photographed at the Royal Kennels, Windsor, 1854. From left to right: Olga, Venus, Pedro, Fatima.*

LEFT: *Group at Balmoral, September 1887. From left to right: Prince Albert Victor of Wales; Princess Alix of Hesse; Queen Victoria; Beatrice, Princess Henry of Battenberg; Princess Irene of Hesse and Basco, Prince Henry of Battenberg's Pug dog.*

ABOVE: *George, Duke of York (later King George V and grandfather to Queen Elizabeth II) with a Pug c1890's.*

Photographs courtesy: The Royal Collection, Her Majesty The Queen.

their mistress. Queen Victoria kept quite a number of Pugs. They were always favourites at Windsor, especially in the Royal nurseries. Some were from the Willoughby strain, others from the Morrison strain and many of these Pugs were imported by Her Majesty herself and the Prince Consort. Among them were Olga, Pedro, Venus, Minika and Fatima, all of which were good examples of the breed, and Venus had puppies. Others were called Mops, Topsy and Duchess. The list is endless. Some names are repeated. Bosco, considered to be a fine specimen of the breed, must have been quite a favourite. In some reports the name is written as Basco, but I am sure it is the same dog. It was once said of him that: "He would at Windsor have taken possession of the throne if he thought that it looked comfortable enough, and been surprised if asked to move." When Bosco died he was buried in Frogmore House Gardens, Windsor. A stone was erected over his grave by Queen Victoria in 1892 and inscribed:

BOSCO
1877 — 1892

On the other side it reads: "Bosco, favourite dog of their Royal Highnesses Prince and Princess of Battenberg". This memorial can still be seen today. The artist Charles Burton Barber painted a water-colour of Bosco, measuring 16.5 by 23.7 cms, which hangs in the Royal Collection at Osborne House.

Queen Victoria always insisted on naming all her dogs herself and particularly the new puppies. She kept an impressive cloth-bound book with the title *Dogs in the Home Park Kennel at Windsor* stamped on it in gold lettering. She was very thorough in recording the name, date of birth, sex and parents of puppies born, and the details of the place and time that she obtained her dogs, together with any other comments about them. This book included many Pugs. Queen Victoria always insisted that all her dogs lived 'as nature gave them to the world', with no cropped ears, no docked tails and no 'faulty' puppies put down.

A contemporary of Bosco was Mistress Rooney, owned by Princess Margaret of Connaught, granddaughter of Queen Victoria. Queen Victoria owned and was very fond of Rooney's daughter Ayah, a silver-grey bitch with many good qualities but not a show dog. She also owned a so-called rough-coated Pug called Quiz, who had a fully feathered tail, and this was some eighteen years before Mr W. Holdsworth brought one out as a 'novelty'. In the past it has been a surprise to discover that Queen Victoria had a black Pug many years before Lady Brassey is reported to have introduced it to this country. Queen Victoria's black Pug had four white feet and a white 'shirt-front' and hideously cropped ears, so he was not of her breeding. In 1886 Queen Victoria received from Lady Brassey a black Pug named Jacopa, a daughter of Jack Spratt and Tragedy and she renamed her Brassey. Most of the information about Queen Victoria's Pugs was reported in the *Ladies' Kennel Journal* in 1896 and was written with reference to a photograph album belonging to the Queen. What happened to this album I do not know. Certainly as such it no longer exists, or at least, if it does, then it is not in the possession of HM Queen Elizabeth in her Royal Collection at Windsor Castle, although some photographs and paintings do exist.

Other members of the Royal household also favoured the Pug. Princess Maud of

Wales, granddaughter of Queen Victoria, had a Pug called Punch who died in 1882. Another, called Bully, was a fawn bitch, who was given to her in 1894 by the Prince of Wales, her father, later Edward VII. Bully went everywhere with her, including Marlborough and Sandringham, and lived until he was nineteen years old. In the *Ladies' Kennel Journal* (May 1895) it was reported that Princess May of Teck, who later became Queen Mary, was given a Pug called Avenue Jack by Mrs Roberts on her visit to the Richmond Show. Then in June 1896 the Princess of Wales, later to become Queen Alexandra, went to the LKA Show. In 1897 Premier Black Gin, owned by the Princess of Wales, was in the parade of Champions at the LKA Show where she is said to have won the first prize in every class she competed in. Black Gin was shown often and won many prizes. She became very attached to Mrs Jackson, the wife of the headkeeper at Sandringham, and stayed there with her. Another of Queen Alexandra's Pugs, Babette, was said to have been very well-bred with a perfect shape and coat. In later years, as I have mentioned, the Duke and Duchess of Windsor had quite a few Pugs, both black and fawn. Now the long line of the Pugs, having been in the Royal household since 1688, has come to an end. Queen Elizabeth II, though obviously a dog-lover, prefers the Corgi and the Labrador.

2 CHOOSING A PUG

Having decided to buy a Pug, be sure you go to a reputable breeder. It is not wise to go to unknown kennels and, most certainly, do not go to a commercial source. To find a reputable breeder, contact the Pug Dog Club in your area. The secretary will be able to give you names, addresses and telephone numbers of breeders. You will probably need to make several telephone calls to find a breeder with a litter of puppies for sale. You may even have to reserve a puppy before it is born and travel farther afield than you had intended, but I can assure you it will all be worthwhile. Don't think for one moment that you can decide that you want a Pug and just go out to buy a good one. It all takes time. Good breeders are very particular in ensuring that their puppies all go to good homes. A breeder with years of experience will be able to help you from the start, and a good breeder will always be there with advice during the lifetime of your Pug.

If you choose a female, you will have to cope with her seasonal cycle.

Photo: Carol Ann Johnson.

The male Pug is similar in temperament to the female, and is a very devoted companion.

Photo: Carol Ann Johnson.

MALE OR FEMALE?

You will need to decide if you want a male or female and the breeder will probably ask your reason for making this choice. From my own point of view I see no difference, it is a matter of opinion. Lots of people think that bitches are closer to their owners but, personally, I have not found this so. With a bitch, seasons have to be contended with, and with a dog there is the problem of him cocking his leg. You may have the cleanest dog imaginable – until friends arrive bringing their dog or bitch with them and, once your Pug smells that dog, there is nothing you can do to stop him wetting. Coping with a bitch in season is not difficult. Tablets can be bought to keep the smell of the season away. That is not to say that if we can't smell a bitch in season, dogs still can but these tablets will discourage them. One has to be very careful when taking a bitch for a walk. A stray dog could follow you to your home and be a nuisance. I would certainly never let a child take a bitch in season for a walk – it is far too risky

for the child and the bitch. If your interest is strictly in having a Pug as a pet, it is worth considering having your dog neutered.

LIAISING WITH THE BREEDER

On making your contact with the breeder you will discuss many details. When the puppies are old enough the breeder will allow you to see them. You may be asked to remove your shoes and, if you are allowed to handle the puppies (and you may not be given this privilege), you may be asked to wash your hands first. All this is to ensure that the puppies are not in contact with any outside infections. When you see the puppies for the first time they should look like a miniature specimen of an adult Pug. Usually they are on their own and the mother is brought in a little later. The breeder will explain to you all you wish to know and will give details of the finer points one needs for a good specimen of the breed. The breeder will describe each puppy's character for, having watched them

28

from birth, she will know them individually; whether one is more boisterous than the others, or one is very quiet. Usually one particular puppy will catch your eye. Point this one out and discuss this puppy with the breeder, who will tell you all about it. Look at the rest of the litter. Watch them running around, playing, notice everything about the puppy you have picked out. You may still come back to your first choice.

There will be so much to talk about. Take the advice of the breeder. It makes no difference if you want your Pug for showing or as a pet – you will want a good, healthy, strong animal. You will get many years of pleasure from this dear little Pug, whose company you can expect for anything up to fourteen years or more. Also, at the breeder's home you will be able to see other members of the Pug family. See how they all behave at home and I am sure that, when you leave, you will long to get

back, a few weeks later, to collect that lovely puppy. If you have any doubts that, on your return, you will not get the puppy you have chosen, the breeder may be willing to mark the puppy in some way. I used to use a little dab of nail varnish under the flap of the ear. At this stage you will be able to discuss the finance of the transaction and you will make an agreement. The breeder will tell you how to feed and rear your puppy, which is most important. Do not be afraid to ask questions. You have a new adventure, being the owner of a Pug. I am sure you will never regret it. Some breeders may suggest having two Pugs from the same litter to keep each other company. This is something I personally wouldn't advise, especially if it happens to be males. It can, and has been known, to cause problems. Maybe, at a later date when your puppy has grown up, you can buy a companion. This seems to be more satisfactory.

When you visit a breeder, you will have the opportunity to see adult Pugs, which will give you some idea of the type of dog that the kennel produces. Photo: Carol Ann Johnson.

PREPARING YOUR HOME

There are many things to consider when preparing your home for the arrival of the new member of the family, for that is what your Pug puppy will be. It is important to make sure that your puppy will have a comfortable bed. There are plenty to select from in the pet shops or at dog shows. It is a matter for your own choice, but I would suggest having changes of cushions or covers that are easily washable. Small travelling boxes also make excellent beds. Put the bed in a draught-free and warm position. Do not put it where someone can fall over it, has to tread over it, or is likely to drop anything on your new puppy. Most people, if keeping their puppy in the kitchen, find that under the kitchen table is ideal.

Your puppy will need a plaything as, at this stage, he or she will be missing their brothers and sisters. There are plenty of toys around to choose from. A rubber bone when puppy is teething and a soft, safe, outgrown baby toy are ideal. It is not necessary to buy anything new, but make sure it is nothing that your puppy can chew, or eat, or is in any way harmful. Chews of all varieties are available. Of course by now you must have bought a collar and lead, a water bowl, a feeding bowl and a brush and comb. I prefer a chain collar (not a choke chain), one that closes together to the size of the Pug's neck, so it is better to wait until you have your puppy before purchasing. Your Pug will eventually grow out of the first one and a larger size will be required. Since this is the kind of collar that will be needed for the show ring, should you decide to show, it is as well to get your dog used to one. At first, a small leather collar is quite useful to put on your puppy to play around. Some puppies object to any collar and so this type could be an early start, but puppies soon grow out of them. Washable nylon leads are by far the best to attach to the chain. Do make sure it has a strong safety catch. I suggest that the feeding bowl is aluminium and about six to seven inches across (approx. 15 to 18 cm). They are by far the best. No chipping, no breaking, and they clean easily. The water bowl should be firm, not one so light that your dog will be chasing it around the room or picking it up and chewing it. I have a heavy earthenware type and have been using the same ones for over thirty years. You can find more details on brushes, combs and nail clippers in my section on grooming. It is hygienic for dogs to have their own towels, even if they are your own discarded ones. Something that I have always found useful for wiping dirty feet is a towelling oven cloth. Your hands fit in firmly and it makes drying easy to deal with.

COLLECTING YOUR PUPPY

Before you leave, it is advisable to obtain from the breeder the pedigree of your puppy and the registration and transfer forms. This really is most important. Also check what inoculations the puppy has had. Once your puppy has said "Goodbye" to mother, brothers and sisters and you have left the breeder, make sure that your puppy is cuddled up and secure for travelling on the journey home. All my puppies used to go home wearing a little coat. I always thought it gave them a secure feeling on the home journey. It is advisable for safety's sake to put your puppy in a small travelling cage. You will, no doubt, be able to borrow one from a friend or the breeder, but you may wish to purchase your own. Try sitting by your puppy so that you can keep a

If you want to show your Pug, the breeder will help you to pick out a puppy with show potential.

watchful eye and give an occasional word of comfort. Do not be surprised if your puppy is car sick. This is not unusual. Remember, this is all a very new and strange experience for this tiny animal. Once home, give your puppy lots of loves and cuddles – but I am sure I have no need to explain that. If possible, try to arrange to collect your puppy during the day so that there is time to get familiar with the new surroundings before bedtime.

ARRIVING HOME
On arriving home put puppy first into the garden. All puppies will certainly want to relieve themselves at this stage. Let the

newcomer smell around the new playground if it wishes, but, of course, it is all bound to feel strange. The puppy will also require a drink. Here again, introduce the new drinking vessel, with probably a little milk. Don't force it – puppies should be allowed to drink only if they want to. Then when you bring your puppy back into the house, introduce the new bed. Then leave the puppy. Do not fuss or keep picking him or her up. I know you will find this hard to resist, but it is better to let your new puppy explore this exciting new home alone. The puppy will, even at this early stage, begin to know the sound of your voice and, before long, will follow you around. Whatever you do, don't start giving treats. Anything in the way of food should be given when the meal is due. Of course, you will want to take your new puppy out to be introduced to all your friends and neighbours. This is fine. Your puppy will probably thoroughly enjoy this. But do keep a firm grip. Pug puppies are very wriggly and easily dropped. Young children should never lift them up, but your Pug will love playing with children on the floor.

No doubt your breeder will give you a diet sheet for your puppy and it is wise to keep to this feeding programme to save any tummy upsets. There is no need to buy lots of different food to try out. If you have your own idea on feeding, then change your puppy's diet gradually. I have described elsewhere in this book how I feed my new puppies and how to feed an adult Pug.

Remember that your puppy is still a baby and will need plenty of sleep, so don't wear your Pug out too much. When bedtime arrives, I advise you to put your puppy into his or her own bed, say "Goodnight", as I always do, and leave. If your puppy starts to cry, ignore it for a short while. If you find the puppy has not settled down, give a little treat and say "Goodnight" again. If this still does not work, you may have to take your puppy into your room, but try to avoid this unless you want to make it a regular habit. Persevere, encourage your puppy to stay in the puppy bed at night. Don't give in unless it is really necessary.

A Pug has a wonderful character which could be spoilt if proper rearing is not done at the puppy stage. A close relationship with the owner and family is most important. A Pug loves a game, plenty of playing. That's why a Pug is so good with children. Talk to your Pug – who really does listen and understand. Oh yes! I know how a Pug can turn a deaf ear when the mood dictates, but change your tone of voice, or say something which will encourage, and the attention of your Pug will soon be drawn to you.

When your puppy first arrives home, stick to the diet that he has been used to in order to avoid stomach upsets.

Photo: Carol Ann Johnson.

3 CARING FOR YOUR PUG

During early puppyhood your puppy will sometimes make a mistake with excitement but, by the time six months of age is reached, a puppy should have learnt to be clean. If a mistake is made, scold with a firm voice. Just one outcry, not a lot of mumble-jumble. Never use your hand to smack a puppy. With a lot of patience you will be rewarded with a clean Pug for the rest of the dog's life. Pugs are intelligent, and will learn very quickly the meaning of the harsh voice that you use when naughty behaviour has occurred. At the same time, praise and make a fuss of your Pug for good behaviour. It is the difference in your tone of voice that distinguishes good from bad.

VACCINATIONS

The breeder should have had your puppy vaccinated against the four major diseases: Distemper, Hepatitis, Leptospirosis and Parvovirus. Check with the breeder whether this has been done. If not, consult your vet as to how to proceed, and make sure that any other precautions, specific to the area in which you live, have been taken. Vaccinations are vital to the health and well-being of your Pug and must be done at an early age. Booster vaccinations are required once a year for the rest of your Pug's life.

EARLY SOCIALISATION AND TRAINING

Having had the inoculations, your puppy is now ready to go out and mix with other dogs. It is useful to take your puppy to a training club run by your local canine society. This will give the puppy the feeling of being handled by other people and the atmosphere of a show, if that is your wish. Watch your puppy carefully. You don't want your puppy to be frightened by, perhaps, a larger breed of puppy at the class. Try to get your puppy used to everything gently and sensibly.

I find the best time to give a little training on a lead, and on the table, is before a meal. A puppy, waking from a sleep, first needs to relieve itself, hopefully in the garden. After a run round, very gently put a small collar around the puppy's neck and have a little play. Attach the lead and attempt to walk. You may find that the puppy is most happy to go – if so, just walk backwards and forwards a few times, then that will do. Don't overdo it. If you have a

A puppy has a lot to get used to when he first arrives in a new home, so be patient with him and give plenty of reassurance.

Photo: Carol Ann Johnson.

puppy that won't move, don't pull, try to encourage. If just three or four steps are managed on the lead, make that do for the first lesson. Always praise and make a fuss. These lessons should only last for about ten minutes, but do them often.

Then try the table. At first do not worry if the puppy's legs are not in the correct position. All you want is for the puppy to stand up on four legs and be happy about it. Place your hand under the body and lift, stroking with the other hand and talking

kindly. Don't forget, at this stage we are talking about a two to three-month-old puppy, and these are the first lessons. Once your puppy stands up, give plenty of praise, show the food bowl, take one piece out and give it to puppy. Lift the puppy down on to the floor to eat. If this is done before each meal the puppy will then associate one with the other, with the meal as a reward. Keep these short exercises going every day – never give up.

Pugs enjoy moderate exercise – although they are not generally fond of water!

EXERCISE

Pugs do not need a lot of exercise. If your Pug has the freedom of a well-fenced in garden, he or she will enjoy a good romp. A garden, or a reasonably-sized patio, is very useful if, for some reason or other, you are unable to go out. A nice sturdy one mile walk during the morning, and another later in the day is beneficial, especially if taken just before a meal, as this rouses the appetite and your Pug will be ready for a rest afterwards. Of course, if the weather is bad, the walk may be shortened. During snow and wet weather, put a coat on your Pug. No, this is not mollycoddling! It is sensible if your Pug has just left a warm room. If in the summer the weather is very warm, do not attempt a long walk. Watch carefully if you are in a park – some dogs are not as friendly as a Pug. Do not let your Pug off the lead where there is traffic, no matter how well trained you think he or she may be, there are always adverse situations that you may not be aware of and which may be dangerous to you, your Pug and other road users.

Generally speaking, Pugs are not fond of water and very few of them will go into the sea of their own accord. No Pug should ever be forced or thrown into water. Because of their heavy body and short nose they might easily be drowned if left to their own resources. Having said this, however, quite a number of Pugs do enjoy a swim. Quite recently I saw a video of Lundi Blamey's Pugs swimming and thoroughly enjoying themselves in a swimming pool in South Africa. I also remember my friend, Norman Wooler, phoning me one day, telling me that Goodchance Eddystone had swum across their local river. He was then about seven months old. I was once asked by a dog agency for a puppy that they could train for the water, as they needed it for the TV film *Swallows and Amazons*. I managed to get a puppy for them who made such a success of it that he was eventually engaged for the part of 'Willie' in the UK soap opera *Eastenders*.

GROOMING

There is really so little to do in the grooming of a Pug that it must be one of the easiest breeds of dog to deal with. No

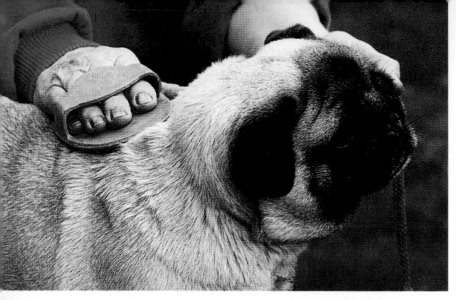

GROOMING ROUTINE

Photos:
Carol Ann Johnson.

Brush the coat briskly, using a stiff brush or a rubber glove.

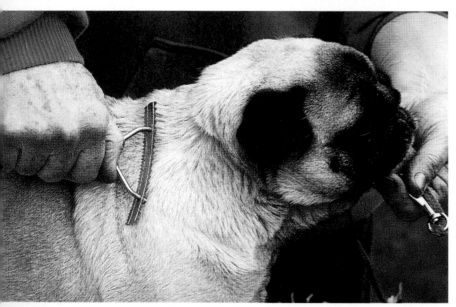

If your Pug is shedding its coat, you may need to comb through using a steel comb.

Finally, give your dog a rub down. You can do this with your hands or with a grooming mitten.

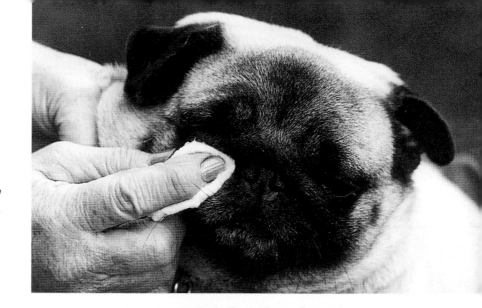

Wipe the eyes with cotton-wool.

Make sure the ears are clean, but be careful not to probe into the ear canal.

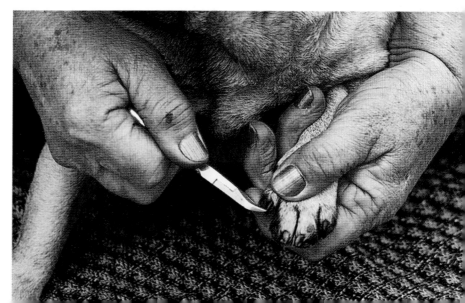

If necessary, trim your Pug's nails, making sure you do not cut into the quick.

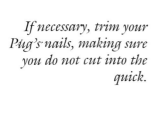

cutting, no trimming, no plucking. How wonderful! In the UK scissors are not used on Pugs, but in the USA whiskers and any surplus hairs are cut away. I read a book recently where the author said "Good grooming starts inside the dog." This takes me back to my very early days in the breed. When I was showing one of my Pugs under the late Mr W. Young (Rydens), he remarked on the lovely coat my Pug had and said to me: "What goes inside an animal shows on the outside." This is so true. A dog having a rich coat, lustrous eyes and external beauty must be clean and wholesome inside.

However, there is still some work to be done for the owner of a Pug. We cannot rely on nature alone. I think the most tiresome thing with a Pug is the shedding of hairs. Now this is something that does need attention. The coat should be brushed quite briskly every day using a stiff brush (or I find a rubber glove useful) and then a combing with a steel comb. Finally give a nice rub down with the hands. Never use a wire brush.

I do not believe in lots of baths. Giving your Pug too many baths will wash away the natural oils which dogs have in their skin for protection. I leave it to your own discretion as to when and how often you think your Pug needs to be bathed. Should your Pug get dirty while playing etc., simply dampen a towel and wipe the dog down, then dry the coat and give it a good brush. I bath my Pugs in a baby bath on a table – and do they love it! They each stand and wait their turn. Make sure you have everything ready: shampoo, plenty of towels, cotton or cotton wool, Vaseline and anything else you may need. While my Pug is sitting in the bath before the wash, I attend to the head: clean the ears with cotton or cotton wool, wipe the eyes (each with a fresh piece of cleaning material), tend to the overnose wrinkle – if dirty, gently clean and powder, then use a little Vaseline if the nose is crusty. When the head has been attended to, I proceed with the wash. I wet the coat all over with water, the temperature as for a baby. I apply the shampoo, lather and rub well over the body, legs and feet. Now for the rinsing: do make sure all the shampoo is completely washed away. Dry thoroughly with a towel or hair dryer if you prefer. If the weather is fine your Pug can run around outdoors, but if it is at all cold, keep the dog indoors until the coat is completely dry.

A Pug's toenails should be kept short. If you can manage to give your Pug plenty of walks on hard ground or a lot of running around on your patio to keep the toenails down, this is by far the best thing, for Pugs do hate having them cut. If you do have to cut them, use special clippers that are sold at dog shows or pet stores and make sure that you do not cut beyond the quick. Pugs, having black toenails, make it difficult to know just where the quick is, so it is very easy to make a mistake and the nail will bleed. Ask your vet for a solution that you can keep by you, should this happen, and then a dab with cotton wool, or cotton, will soon stop it.

FEEDING ADULT PUGS

Feeding Pugs is really quite easy but, since most Pugs are greedy, great care should be taken not to overfeed. Just how much food is required depends on your Pug, for there are a number of factors to consider – the dog's size, physical condition, appetite, whether you feed once or twice a day and whether the food you give contains the correct vitamins. Just like people, some dogs put on weight rapidly, while others remain slim. One really must study one's own dog's requirements. A Pug that is boisterous and full of energy will need more food than a lazy one who is quite content to lie down and sleep. All these things should be considered. I believe that, if possible, your dog should be fed more or less at about the same time each day, for your Pug will know just when it is time for dinner. My dogs are usually fed once a day between five and seven o'clock. My reason for this is that, if I go to a show, or out visiting or shopping, or if for any other reason I am away from home during the day, I can make sure I am back for feeding time. My Pugs have a saucer of milk and a piece of toast for breakfast and before they go to bed they have another drink of milk. One thing I do disagree with is giving dogs treats from your table. If your dog is trained not to expect this, then you will not be bothered by a dog worrying you when you are eating.

A daily diet of cooked beef, chicken or fish with a little liver and perhaps a tablespoon of tinned meat, weighing in all about eight to ten ounces, together with a handful of biscuits, is sufficient for an adult Pug. Over the last few years manufacturers have introduced a complete dry food diet, so many breeders have taken to this method of feeding. It is certainly an easy, quick way of dealing with a family of dogs, and I understand it is very successful, but it isn't for me. The meal may serve the purpose as far as vitamins are concerned but it lacks the different tastes to the palate, so surely, in my view, it must be very boring to a dog. I don't think I would like to sit down to a plate of biscuits instead of a roast dinner. I like to think my Pugs eat as I would eat. Therefore I stick to the old

method. Make sure there is always fresh, clean water available. I am not in favour of medicines and tablets etc. unless they are really necessary. My dogs have two yeast tablets a day and during the winter months my 'oldies' have halibut oil capsules.

OLDIES

Having talked about the puppies, the adults and the show Pugs, what about the 'oldies', the ones who have given us so much joy in their younger days? I know that there are quite a number of breeders who find homes for their Pugs which they now class as 'passengers'. In doing this they replace them with a new puppy to show. Providing they are found good homes, all is well. Otherwise they could eventually be handed over to the rescue groups to deal with. Personally I, and many others like me, cannot do this. My Pugs stay with me always, and nearly all have lived long lives.

We do not notice our Pugs ageing until perhaps they no longer get up into the armchair or they cannot get down alone. They prefer to be in their bed. Their walks get shorter. Things begin to go wrong. Visits to the vet become regular. Lots of care is needed. The years are passing – 12, 13, 14! They are still very dear to us and, as long as they are not suffering, or they are not in pain, they live their life through. But we all know what we have to face. No matter how many Pugs we may have had, each one is a special individual and their death is a bereavement difficult to come to terms with. Take good care of them as long as you can. Make sure they are kept warm, are given good nourishing food and a nice bed. Do all you can. They have earned it for all the love you have shared together.

4 *HEALTH CARE*

There are many books that can be obtained for information on first aid for your dog. I do not profess to be an expert on ailments but can only give you an idea of how I have acted in an emergency. It is important to stress that this is *first aid*. After coping with the immediate situation, you should always seek veterinary advice as soon as possible.

FIRST AID
I find it useful to have a first aid kit handy for my Pugs. Its contents include:-

    Benzyl Benzoate
    Bicarbonate of Soda
    Chloromycetin
    Kaolin
    Liquid Paraffin
    Milk of Magnesia – liquid or tablets
    Salt
    Soothing ointment.

Anything used must be thrown away and replaced, so that it is fresh. I don't keep any opened ointments after a month.

I am a firm believer in using a saline solution for such things as cleansing wounds and easing sprains. I might add that this applies to my human family as well as my Pugs. In all circumstances my first reaction is to pick up my Pug to give comfort while examining the dog to see what the problem might be. There is a current trend for alternative medicine such as herbal and homoeopathic remedies but, in my opinion, this is a subject for people experienced in these matters, not for the layman such as me although I have tried a few of these remedies on my own Pugs. If you are interested in using them I suggest that you consult a professional. This is not to say that I believe in the use of too many hard drugs; I just prefer to rely on simple remedies.

BEE AND WASP STINGS
If possible remove the bee sting, perhaps using a pair of tweezers. Wasps do not leave their sting. Swab with bicarbonate of soda, one teaspoon to a cup of water, or apply a raw onion. If the sting is on the lips or in the mouth, swab frequently using cotton wool, or cotton, soaked in spirits such as whisky or methylated spirits. From my own experience I put ice in the mouth to keep the swelling down. If the sting is in the throat, immediate veterinary help is essential. Antihistamine treatment will be administered and will give quick relief.

BURNS

If your Pug receives a burn, immediately sponge it with cold water. I would then cover it with bicarbonate of soda. Take great care if your Pug spends a lot of time in the kitchen with you where there are hot kettles and saucepans. It is so easy for accidents to happen.

CAR SICKNESS

Some Pugs do suffer from car sickness, especially a puppy on the first car journey. If this persists, tablets can be bought to deal with it.

COLLAPSE

Pugs, as with many flat-nosed dogs, sometimes collapse, usually if they get very excited. This is obviously very frightening for the owner. The dog draws back the palate which cuts off its breathing. This causes the dog to collapse, as in a faint, sometimes crying in fright. After a few seconds the dog will come round and behave as if nothing had happened. It is better to keep your Pug quiet for a while, if this occurs.

CONSTIPATION

When you notice that your Pug has not passed a motion for a short period, administer a little liquid paraffin. If there is no change and you are still worried after a few days, consult your vet.

CUTS AND BRUISES

Injuries such as cuts and bruises should first be cleaned with a saline solution. Then you should apply a soothing skin cream.

CYSTS

For cysts between the toes, bathe them in a saline solution to keep them clean. Do this

When you take on a Pug, you are responsible for his health and well-being throughout his life. Photo: Carol Ann Johnson.

often; it will soften the skin and the cyst will burst and be cleansed.

DIARRHOEA

In cases of diarrhoea, cut down on the food you are giving your Pug. Give the dog one 5ml. spoonful (teaspoon) of Kaolin twice a day. Don't let the condition last any longer than three days. If it persists for longer than that, it is time then to consult your vet.

EYE INJURY

Great care must be taken of a Pug's eyes. First bathe the injury with warm water, then apply Chloromycetin from a fresh tube. You can only get this from your vet.

FITS AND HYSTERIA

If your Pug is having a fit, immediately pick the dog up, using great care in handling. Apply a cold sponge to the head and the back of the neck. Keep the Pug in a warm, darkened room to rest quietly. If you experience this with your Pug, and it is the first occurrence, I would suggest that you consult your vet who may treat the problem.

GRASS EATING

If you find that your Pug is continually eating grass, this signals some form of digestive problem. From my personal experience I would give my Pug a Milk of Magnesia tablet to correct the problem.

NETTLE RASH

When nettle rash occurs, it is usually noticed that, quite suddenly, your Pug is covered with raised blotches. The skin over the head may present an almost quilted appearance and swelling of the gums or throat may cause some discomfort. Milk of Magnesia liquid given directly is a great help. In many cases the symptoms disappear spontaneously, after a few hours, but they may return again. If this is the first occurrence you may wish to consult your vet, who will prescribe antihistamine treatment which will usually give quick relief from the symptoms.

POISONING

If you suspect poisoning, give your Pug one tablespoonful of salt in warm water to make the dog vomit. Then consult your vet. It is easier to treat if you know what poison has been consumed. Of course, keep all medicines, your own included, out of reach of your Pugs, just as you would keep them out of the reach of children. Watch out for the unexpected rat and mouse poisons, and garden insecticides and weed killers.

SPRAINED LEG

Should your Pug be limping and, after close examination, you don't know why, bathe the affected area in a saline solution of two tablespoonfuls of salt in a small bowl of warm water. Place the leg in the solution for about fifteen minutes and repeat fairly often. If there is no improvement after a day or so, ask your vet to determine the cause of lameness and treat it accordingly.

COMMON AILMENTS
ANAL GLANDS

On either side of the anus of both dogs and bitches is situated an anal gland. These are scent glands which produce a very foul-smelling secretion. In the wild, this was originally a lubricant that better enabled the dog to pass faeces, but with modern-day feeding this is not necessary. These glands have a tendency to get clogged and a fetid mass accumulates in them. This accumulation is not, strictly speaking, a disease – unless it becomes infected and purulent. A dog whose anal glands are in need of attention will exhibit considerable irritation and discomfort, sliding along the ground on its bottom or licking and biting continually under the tail. Almost all dogs and bitches have some accumulation which need not have serious consequences. However, it is better if the glands are relieved. Some owners are able to empty these themselves, but get your vet to do it if you are not sure how.

CHEYLETIELLA

The Cheyletiella mite is minute, it cannot

be seen with the naked eye. Usually we only know that our dog has the mite in its coat when we ourselves come out in a scabious type cluster of spots with great irritation. It does not affect everyone. My husband never had any effect from it, but I did, and it is most unpleasant but nothing to be alarmed about. Give your Pug a good bath with an insecticide shampoo, and as for yourself, apply a dab of insect cream when itching is uncomfortable and it will go in a couple of days.

ECLAMPSIA

Eclampsia is due to a calcium deficiency in bitches either in the later stage of pregnancy or just after whelping. The bitch may become unsteady and collapse. Consult your vet immediately, who will give the bitch an injection. All this can be avoided by giving your bitch sufficient calcium and vitamins during pregnancy and while nursing puppies.

ECZEMA

Eczema is a non-contagious disease which is common in dogs. There are two types: dry eczema shows itself in scurfy, scaly and cracked inflamed patches; wet eczema is patches of wet raw skin sores. It affects the back, principally at the front of the tail; the head and face, especially the edges of the lips and the eyes; the flaps of the ears and sometimes inside the ears. Dry eczema often appears between the thighs. Constant licking can spread the infection to the lips, which are difficult to heal. There is irritation and itching. The dog scratches, bites and scrapes at the affected areas. The pain may cause your dog to resent being handled. The condition may be hereditary or it may be caused by a faulty diet resulting in a deficiency of vitamins and/or

minerals. It could be due to disturbance brought about by overfeeding, particularly with sugars and starches, or it could be caused by worms. Consult your vet for advice on this matter.

EYE ULCERS

These are actually injuries to the eye surface and they are common in Pugs because of their typically prominent eyes. Consult your vet as soon as possible, as these are not only very painful but can lead to complete loss of sight in the affected eye. It is most important to stop your Pug from scratching at the eye and making the condition worse.

FALSE PREGNANCY

Many bitches, even maiden bitches, show symptoms of the condition known as 'false pregnancy' between six to eight weeks after a season. They may secrete a quantity of milk and even show signs of some abdominal swelling. If this goes on without treatment to the ninth week the bitch will suffer great discomfort. She roams about whining and crying. She scrapes up her bed and, if in the house, the carpets and seats of chairs, twisting about as if trying to make a nest for the phantom puppies. She may even carry a doll or a woolly toy about. All this is due to the normal reactions of the bitch to the actions of her hormones. There is no need to worry. It is thought by many that a bitch should have a litter of puppies to stop this, but it is not true. This condition can be cured with surprising rapidity by one or two tablets containing Stilboestrol, which your vet can prescribe. Stilboestrol treatment should be under professional supervision, as overdosing may affect the womb in later life. The best advice I got from a vet many years ago was to let nature take care of itself, and that is what I have done since. I cut down on liquids to a minimum. If a bitch going through a false pregnancy refuses food, I do not worry unduly. This will all help to dry up the milk. Take her for plenty of walks – anything to take her mind off brooding. It will pass.

KENNEL COUGH

This is a persistent, infectious cough which occurs most commonly under kennel conditions. It is highly contagious and a dog with Kennel Cough should never be allowed to mix with other dogs for several weeks. As a rule the dog does not seem ill and recovers quite quickly. If any complications develop, your vet should be consulted.

MANGE

There are two types of Mange, Demodectic and Sarcoptic. Some years ago Demodectic Mange was common in Pugs. Even though breeders and owners never spoke about this problem, it didn't mean that this wasn't present at the time – nor would it go away by hiding the fact. My experience with Demodectic Mange occurred many years ago with a young puppy that I had bought. I had no idea what I was dealing with at first because I was ignorant of the disease. A small spot on top of the puppy's head would not go away, much as I tried with various ointments. I decided on a visit to the vet, who informed me that it was mange and pointed out other spots that I had not noticed. It took time but my puppy was cured and it never returned. I believe mange becomes generalised because the owner does not know the significance of the first small spot and so the condition goes unnoticed. Demodectic Mange is caused by a parasite which lives not only on the skin but also in the bloodstream and the lymphatic glands. Hence it should be treated both internally as well as on the surface. It is not contagious but it can be hereditary. A dab of Benzyl Benzoate, bought from any chemist, dabbed on a suspected spot is a great help.

Sarcoptic mange is caused by a parasite and is highly contagious to other dogs and sometimes to humans. It is not hereditary and it does need veterinary attention. The first sign is irritation, and it usually appears around the eyes, elbows, hocks and abdomen. The hair drops out in patches. The affected area is covered with small spots resembling flea bites.

OTITIS (CANKER)

Parasitic infection with the ear mite otodectes causes intense irritation. As a result the dog scratches and shakes its head, causing small injuries to the inner surface of the ear. Bacterial infection follows and if treatment is not given promptly the result may be a very prolonged and intractable case of ear trouble. Pugs are no more prone to ear canker or aural trouble than any other dog, but care must be taken of the ears. It is wise to take precautions by putting a pinch of boracic powder inside the ear once a week, thus cleansing and soothing the ears. Always avoid letting any water enter the ears at bath times.

PYOMETRA

Pyometra is a very common condition affecting the uterus or womb of bitches, in the period up to nine weeks after a season. It is most common in middle-aged bitches, but it can occur even after the first season. A bitch suffering with Pyometra usually develops a very marked thirst. She may be listless and will vomit in the later stages.

Her temperature is raised and she develops such a distended abdomen that the owner may suspect that she is having puppies. In the case of Open Pyometra the cervix, or neck of the uterus, remains open and the discharge is overflowing and draining away all the time. Usually the first symptoms that the owner notices are that the bitch is constantly cleaning herself, as if she were in season, and she usually has a pronounced thirst. Although Open Pyometra is less sudden in onset, it is still almost invariably fatal if not treated. If your bitch is showing any of the symptoms mentioned, consult your vet as soon as possible. Postponement of even a few days could cost your pet's life. In nearly all cases a hysterectomy is needed, together with antibiotic treatment. Do not delay in visiting your vet through dread of an operation – with modern methods of anaesthesia and tranquillisers your pet will suffer no pain or distress. There is a mistaken idea that allowing a bitch to have a litter of puppies will prevent her from developing Pyometra. This is not true. The only way of preventing this condition is by sterilising the bitch early in life.

UMBILICAL HERNIA
An Umbilical Hernia is formed at birth from a failure of the abdominal wall to heal over completely at the umbilicus. A very small umbilical hernia may do no harm but it is wiser to consult your vet in case an operation is necessary.

VACCINATIONS
All canines should be vaccinated against the four major diseases, Distemper, Hepatitis, Leptospirosis and Parvovirus by the time they are three months old. Two vaccinations are required in order to provide initial protection for a full year.

Regular annual booster vaccinations against these diseases are essential. A Record of Vaccination, available from your vet, is an important document that should be kept safe and readily available. Adult dogs can also be vaccinated against Parainfluenza and Bordetellosis.

WORMING
All dogs should be wormed regularly every six months. Worms can cause problems so it is far better to be safe than sorry. Modern medicines can easily solve the problem.

HEREDITARY CONDITIONS
When owning and, especially, breeding dogs, one must always be aware of any hereditary defects that could be troublesome to you and your dog, so this chapter is not meant to scare you but just to put you in the picture as to what could happen. Fortunately the majority of breeders do take precautions and any Pug who is suspected of having a hereditary defect is withdrawn from breeding and so we are able to prevent the defect becoming widespread. Do bear in mind that what is written here are few-and-far-between cases, but if you are seriously interested in the breed it is as well to know what can happen.

CLEFT PALATE
Cleft palate describes the failure of the two halves of the palate in the roof of the mouth to fuse together during development before birth. Puppies born with this condition should be put to sleep as soon as possible without the mother seeing them.

ENTROPION
Entropion is uncommon in Pugs but I have

heard of one or two cases in recent years. This is a congenital condition where either the top, bottom or both eyelids turn inwards, causing the eyelashes to continually rub on the eyeball. This will cause irritation to the cornea, weeping and eventually, if not treated, blindness. So if you suspect this condition, consult your vet who will be able to perform a corrective operation.

HEMI-VERTEBRA

More recently we have had cases of a condition known as 'Wedged' or 'Hemi' Vertebra occurring in a number of breeds, including the Pug. This is a congenital spinal deformity which arises from abnormal development of some bones in the spine as a result of asymmetric (one-sided) development or the failure of both growth centres in the vertebra to join. This problem does not usually show itself until the puppy is four to six months old. X-rays have revealed the cause to be malformed vertebrae just behind the shoulders in the area technically described as T.7-9. As the puppy grows, the deformed and misaligned vertebrae interfere with the nerves controlling the hindquarters. It has been known for some puppies to be treated by acupuncture, sometimes having homeopathic remedies at the same time. Eventually the puppies have regained some use of their legs and have been able to lead a near-normal life. However, the condition may lie dormant, as it has been known for the symptoms to appear later in life. It is not positively clear if this is a hereditary condition but it is causing great concern to breeders. It is being dealt with, and a very watchful eye is being kept on the situation. We do not let any troubles go unnoticed.

Great care is taken. It is wise, however, not to breed from lines where there are suspects.

HIP DYSPLASIA

When I first started in Pugs there were a number of cases of Hip Dysplasia. The first symptom of this condition is a poor action of the hindquarters or lameness. It is advisable to have an X-ray examination of the joint which connects the femur (the long bone of the leg) to the pelvis. This is a 'ball and socket' joint, where the head of the femur is shaped like a ball which sits in the acetabulum, the deep socket of the pelvis. With Hip Dysplasia, the head of the femur is malformed and does not fit into the socket joint properly, thus allowing it to move excessively. This condition is incurable and the walk will never be completely normal. In later life there may be paralysis. In some cases an operation to remove the head of the femur may be helpful. Hip Dysplasia has been recognised more in recent years. It generally causes more anxiety to breeders of larger dogs than smaller ones such as the Pug.

LEGG-PERTHES DISEASE

Over the years we have had instances of Legg-Perthes disease, which is the breakdown of the femoral head when the bone decays.

SLIPPING PATELLA (PATELLA LUXATION)

This is a dislocation of the kneecap which can occur in one or both hind legs. Sometimes the joint can be heard clicking as the dog moves. It is a hereditary disease and no dog with this condition should be bred from.

5 TRAINING AND SHOWING YOUR PUG

If you have bought your Pug with the intention of showing, you must spend some time in training. Don't wait until the dog is old enough to be entered for a show and then expect a correct performance on the day. So many good Pugs are not shown to their advantage because of bad handling. Now, where do you start? You must first study your Pug and its character. All Pugs are, without doubt, individuals and each will want to be handled in their own way. Some walk quicker than others, some enjoy showing more than others and some are naughty no matter how you try to make them behave, but if you want to show your Pug, then the dog must be taught.

Firstly your new puppy should have gone through the early stages of training as explained in Chapter Three. Your work does begin at home and all with kindness. It is no use getting annoyed if your Pug doesn't do the right thing. The more gentle you are, and the more kind words spoken, the better results you will get. Talk to your Pug all the time – all dogs love to be spoken to, and they will learn to understand just what you want. From then on, practise as much as you can, but only

for short periods. Walk your dog in the garden just as you would in a show ring. This is not always as simple as it sounds: some dogs will pull. If this happens, try walking slower. Give commands such as "Steady" with a firm voice and a slight tug on the lead. Keep practising this over and over again until your Pug associates the word "Steady" with the tug which will be disliked. Sooner or later your Pug will understand. As soon as a good job is made of this exercise, give plenty of praise, a little reward and leave it at that. This lesson can be given as often as you like but only for short periods. Don't overdo it. Stop immediately your Pug does the lesson satisfactorily. Give lots of praise and finish. Do not hold the lead tight (the term is 'stringing up'); this is no use at all. It will not show the true movement of the Pug. Instead your Pug will pace and lose that unique roll of the breed. (Pacing is a faulty movement in which the left foreleg and left hindleg advance in unison, then the right foreleg and the right hindleg.)

Attend a handling class if you can. This is most useful for atmosphere, but try to keep your dog's attention all the time. If you find there is too much interest being shown

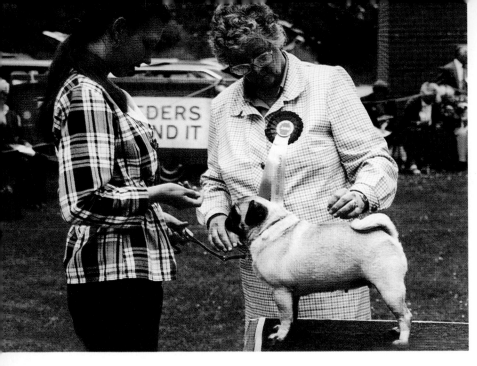

The show Pug must be trained to show himself off to advantage.

Photo: Carol Ann Johnson.

in everything that is going on around you both, then take your Pug's favourite toy to classes with you. This will always get your dog's attention. Don't use a squeaky toy. It is not really good for your dog and is certainly very bad for others. Yes, a tasty morsel if necessary, I see no harm in that, but personally I do dislike handlers with bags of meat dangling in front of their dogs. I like to keep my treat in my pocket and fiddle with it. Puppy sees the movement and watches to see when your hand comes out of the pocket. While this is happening I am constantly talking to my Pug with the word "Stay", a harsh grunt if there is movement, then a gentle "Stay" again and again. Occasionally, take a small treat out of your pocket and give it saying "Good dog", "Good boy" or "Good girl" as you wish. As your puppy grows you will find the stay will last longer. Once your puppy has learnt your command, be sure that the posture is correct.

Pugs, as with all Toy or small dogs, are judged on the table. The reason for this is that it is easier for the judge to get a closer examination. Place your Pug on the table with the head looking outwards. Again, train the dog to stand still and correctly. You may stack your dog by placing the legs in position or, with a little encouragement and good training, your Pug will stand correctly by itself. Always keep hold of the lead, making sure it is not in the way of the Pug or the judge. After all, when the judge turns to look, you will want to show a good balanced specimen of a Pug. The judge will feel the bone on your Pug's legs and body, the texture of the coat and examine the feet, eyes and ears so that he or she gets a good impression of your Pug. The judge does not open a Pug's mouth to see the teeth. This doesn't mean that he must not. If the judge wishes to do this he may, but it is most difficult to open a Pug's mouth to look at teeth for judging assessment. It is far easier just to raise the lip, or run a finger along the teeth. The judge may ask you the age of your Pug. Be ready with the answer. Having been over your dog, the judge will ask you to walk. Before you set off, do make sure your dog is ready to go. This is most important because, if the start isn't correct, then the walk will not be at its best. Here again I always speak to my dog, simply saying "Ready". Then, when your Pug is ready and still, say "Good dog" and start to walk. If the walk becomes a pull or is untidy, stop and make a fresh start. Never carry on with a dog pulling.

Once the judge has seen your Pug you go back to the end of the waiting line. Tell your dog he or she has been good, wriggle the treat in your pocket and give it to your Pug. When the judge is going over the last exhibit, get your Pug in a good standing position. (Practise this by standing in front of a mirror at home.) Make sure you are not too close to other exhibits on either side. Give yourself plenty of room. Now comes the result of your good training and hard work. Occasionally repeat "Stay", and get your dog's whole attention. I find raising the treat to my own mouth encourages the dog to look up, and the anticipation of getting a little of what I have got in my mouth gives a Pug that wide-eyed look and the deep wrinkles show. Try not to bend over your Pug, lowering yourself to your dog's level. It is far better to keep yourself upright. Train your dog to look up at you. All this comes with practice and no matter how old your dog is, a little training before a show will still be required.

A good time and place to train your dog is at a show when judging has finished in a ring. Perhaps you are waiting to go home or to see Best in Show. Make use of your time and the empty rings. The table is there ready, there is plenty of room to move, the atmosphere of the show is all around you and, if necessary, a friend is there to go over your dog, acting as a judge.

I ran a handling class myself for a number of years and trained mostly small or toy

dogs. Each week, as members came, I would ask if they had any problems with their dog and, if they did, I would work hard on that one thing until the dog got it correct. My club earned a good reputation for producing well-trained dogs for the show ring. With this experience in mind I have tried to think of some of the questions that I was frequently asked.

"My dog is afraid of the judge. He walks away from him but on the return he will stand two or three feet away." I trained dogs with this problem quite successfully by walking towards the dog, then gradually stepping backwards, encouraging the dog to follow. I would also change my position. After seeing the dog off on the first outward journey, I would quickly go to the other end of the hall and meet the dog on the way up. Then reverse. The handler must give words of encouragement all the time. Your dog will soon get over this problem.

"My dog does not like the table." There is only one way to deal with this. Practise whenever you can and as often as you can. At home, at shows and at handling classes, put your dog on the table. Give lots of encouragement. Whenever possible ask someone gently to go over your dog as judge while, at the same time, you talk to your dog. Keep at it over and over again. No forcing, no grumbling, just words of comfort.

"My dog keeps sniffing the ground." Yes this is quite a problem. One way of trying, and I do say *trying* to overcome this is to put a little perfume, or anything with a strong smell, on the tip of the nose, which will keep your Pug occupied with curiosity for the amount of time you need. Other than that, and by far the best method, is to train your dog to gait with its head up.

Give a sharp pull of the lead upwards and, at the same time, give a deep grunt, "Up". Your dog will soon link the two responses with each other so that, eventually, just the one word will work.

"My dog keeps chasing the dog in front." This is another problem that is hard to solve. My only suggestion is to try being the leader.

So, if your Pug has any particular problems, speak to the trainer for help. That is what they are there for. All you need to train your Pug is a little time, patience and a good relationship with your dog.

SHOWING

Having trained your dog for showing it is advisable to buy a publication which will supply you with details of shows, their dates and their venues. I would advise you, in England, to try first showing at an Exemption Show, where your dog can be entered on the day and there is a relaxed atmosphere. Every country has its equivalent to this – in the US it is the Match Show. Often these shows are run to raise money on behalf of charities.

You may want to enter an Open show where classes will be scheduled for individual breeds such as Pugs. Many Dog Societies and Breed Clubs run a Limited Show for members only. It is quite easy to join one of these societies. In the case of a breed Club it will be necessary for you to be proposed and seconded by current members. You will find joining such a Club most interesting. All Pugs must be registered before they can be shown and they are not permitted to be shown under six months of age.

BRITISH CHAMPIONSHIP SHOWS

Championship shows are the most prestigious shows of all. In other chapters I have explained the different procedures which apply in different countries but here I will use what happens in the UK as an example. The Kennel Club offers Challenge Certificates (CCs) at Championship Shows of their selection. Most breed clubs are issued with one set per year. General Championship Shows are issued with CCs according to the number of registrations of

Ellen Brown going over an exhibit. The judge's task is to assess each dog against the Breed Standard – the written blueprint of the breed. ·

litters in each breed and the locality of the shows. There are twenty-eight different classes that could be scheduled for a show, but the usual number is fourteen. These are: Minor Puppy (six to nine months); Puppy (nine to twelve months); Junior (twelve to eighteen months); Novice (not having won a CC or three or more first prizes in higher classes at Open or Championship Shows); Post Graduate (not having won a CC or five or more first prizes in Post Graduate or higher classes at Open or Championship Shows); Limit (not having won three CCs or seven or more first prizes in Limit or Open Classes at Championship Shows); and Open (for all dogs of the breed eligible for entry at the show). Winners for each class then challenge for Best Dog, who is awarded a CC. The runner-up is awarded a Reserve CC. The same classes apply for bitches and again the winners of each class challenge, this time for Best Bitch. She receives a CC and the runner-up the Res. CC. The Best Dog and Best Bitch then challenge for Best of Breed. This exhibit then enters for the Group judging. There are six groups; Hound, Gundog, Terrier, Utility, Working and Toy. Winners of each Group challenge for Best in Show.

MAKING UP A BRITISH CHAMPION

Again the regulations vary slightly from country to country and these I have detailed where appropriate. In the UK the Kennel Club is the governing body of dogs and dog shows. The Breed Standards set up by the individual Breed Clubs are approved by the KC. All Breed Clubs are permitted by the KC to hold a Championship, Open and Limited Show each year, for which a licence must be applied. There are twenty-five All-Breed Championship Shows held

each year around the country, plus Group and Breed Championship Shows. It is only at Championship Shows that Challenge Certificates (CC) can be awarded. A Pug awarded three CCs under three different judges carries the title of Champion. At least one of these CCs must be awarded after the age of one year.

NORTH AMERICA

The American Kennel Club and the Canadian Kennel Club regulate dog shows in the USA and Canada. Shows are either All Breed Championship Shows, or Specialty Shows, which are for one breed only. Championship points can be gained at both types of show.

Shows are awarded points, according to the number of dogs of the sex and the breed present. Depending upon the location and entry, the points range from 1 to 5, and American shows giving 3, 4 or 5 points are termed 'majors'. All points count towards the title Champion. In the USA to become a Champion a dog must gain 15 points, with at least two majors under two different judges, and at least a one point win under another judge. In Canada, dogs must win a total of 10 points to become Champions. Majors are not required.

Classes are similar to those of Britain, but Champions enter a separate class for Best of Breed. After the Open class all the unbeaten males compete for 'Winners Dog' and it is this dog who gains the points. The same applies to the bitches, and then Winners Dog and Winners Bitch compete for Best of Winners. Finally, after Best of Breed has been selected, an award is made for Best of Opposite Sex after Best of Winners has been selected. Each Best of Breed competes in its Group, as in the UK, but in the US and Canada there are seven

Groups: Sporting, Hound, Working, Terrier, Toy, Non-Sporting, and Herding.

OBEDIENCE

Very few people think of taking their Pugs for Obedience training, which is quite a pity because a Pug can be as good as any other breed. I'm not saying that one could reach Championship level, not many Toy Dogs ever have, but for enjoyment and pleasure a Pug can be quite successful. I have been responsible for the Obedience section of the South Eastern Counties Toy Dog Society for nearly thirty years. This is the only Society in England to give Obedience classes solely for Toy Dogs. Until I entered my black Pug Satchmo in this show in 1965 no Pug had even competed. Since then I can name only five more. My reason for training Satchmo was because I wanted to give him an interest. My other Pugs were attending shows, but Satchmo did not quite make the grade.

I found a training school and went with great enthusiasm. I was sitting with Satchmo on my lap when the trainer approached me saying "If you want to train your dog in Obedience, you won't do much good if that's how you treat him." I soon made a quick exit. At another school I asked if I was compelled to use a choke chain. This trainer said "I don't mind what you use if you think you can manage it." So here I stayed. I later found another club which trained small dogs only, so every week we attended both clubs.

Firstly Satchmo had to learn to walk at heel. This was quite easy as he was a steady walker. Then he had to learn to sit when I stopped. I encouraged him with just a little

Satchmo with his Obedience awards.   *Owned and trained by Ellen Brown.*

pressure on the hindquarters and a firm word of command, "Sit". With lots of practice at home, this was achieved. Then we had to learn to 'leave your dog'. With Satchmo sitting on the left side of me I would give a last command, "Sit and stay". I would walk away, just a yard or two at first, continually telling him to stay. Then I went back to him. The distance was gradually increased. Next he had to learn to come when called. He was left sitting while I went to the end of the room. When the steward gave me the word, I was to call Satchmo and he had to come towards me and sit in front of me. To finish that exercise he had to walk round the back of me and sit on my left side.

The next lesson was recall with a dumbbell. Satchmo would sit on my left side. I would throw the dumbbell and when I said "Fetch" he would go off and carry it back and sit in front of me. On the steward's command I would take the dumbbell from him. I would tell Satchmo to "Finish" and he would sit on my left side. This took quite a lot of training. Firstly I had to get a dumbbell to suit his mouth, both in size and weight. This is most important. Those on sale didn't quite work. Either they were too heavy, or they were too short. So I had one specially made for him. To keep him holding it in his mouth was really hard work, with me constantly saying, over and over again, "Hold, hold, hold". The first time he did manage it the whole training club gave a cheer.

From those early lessons Satchmo went on to higher classes. Nothing would have been achieved without lots of practice, encouragement and kindness. Both Satchmo and I enjoyed every moment of it. At class he would walk into the hall as if he

Merry with the South Eastern Counties Toy Dog Society's Sebastian Cup for Obedience, 1992. Owned and trained by Pamela Dawe.

owned it. He was very popular with everyone. We never took the work too seriously, I didn't want to. It was just meant to be fun, and this is why Satchmo was so good when it came to competitive work. He did it to please me – such was the love and devotion we had for each other. I firmly believe that this can only be achieved by love and kindness, with lots of patience from the owner. There is nothing cruel or demanding as is sometimes said. I never demanded anything of him. I simply taught him and then asked him to do it and he understood and enjoyed it. Satchmo was the most lovable and devoted Pug anyone could wish to own. Training a dog in obedience brings out its intelligence and that certain link between owner and dog.

Our club would often be asked to give demonstrations at carnivals and fetes, and to our trainer Satchmo was a must. He provided the audience with all that they wanted. His work was good but, if mistakes were made, it was Satchmo who gave the laughs and enjoyment. To see him sitting in the centre of a large field between a German Shepherd Dog and a Golden Retriever gave a laugh to start with, but he loved it. As he was the smallest dog in training he always had to be leader, and this he did with pomp. In the early days of the Pug Dog Club garden parties, which were held at Mrs Greenwood's home at Two Ponds in Crookham, Hampshire, Satchmo would give a display of his work – much to the enjoyment of our members. He loved it and they loved it.

I remember one very interesting show when another Pug entered. Up to then Satchmo seemed to be the only Pug in Britain doing competitive work, now he had opposition. The new Pug was Jiminy Jonah Jizzle, a fawn owned by Mrs Mayo. The first test came, placings were J.J.J. 1st, Satchmo 2nd (he had some crooked sits). In the next class they changed places – Satchmo was 1st, J.J.J. was 2nd (he had crooked sits and played with his retrieving article). Still what an achievement for both

Pugs when there were many other Toy breeds in the class. Mrs Pengally was another competitor who entered Obedience classes and performed very well with a fawn Pug by the name of Brakenvan Danny Boy, who won many awards. Another frequent competitor was Pamela Dawe and her Pug, Merry of Pretty Corner, who was most successful in her classes, often going away with prizes. Pamela said that Merry was the most intelligent Pug that she had had the pleasure of owning in twenty years.

In 1985 a black Pug named Sooty helped to raise £3000 for Charity in three years. He was awarded a special presentation by the Chaplain of the trust, who said, "A dog loves you more than you love yourself and that's a tremendous lot." The money was collected by flag days when Sooty would shake the hand of donors. He also raised money through sponsored events in Obedience.

I have known one or two more owners who have trained their Pugs but they are very few and far between. Obedience training with a Pug is most enjoyable and rewarding and I would like to encourage anyone who is training or thinking of training a Pug. I hope you enjoy it as much as myself and Satchmo and the other Pugs and owners mentioned here. It is such a pity that more are not trained.

6 THE BREED STANDARDS

The purpose of the Breed Standard is that it is a guide to the conformation of the dog. Each part of the anatomy is individually explained as to what is required for perfection and as to the points to look for when buying, showing, breeding and judging. The British Breed Standard has been accepted by the Kennel Club from the English breeders and is the basis for the Pug Standard used, with slight changes in emphasis, throughout America and most countries in the world.

THE BRITISH BREED STANDARD

GENERAL APPEARANCE Decidedly square and cobby, it is 'multum in parvo', shown in compactness of form, well knit proportions and hardness of muscle.

CHARACTERISTICS Great charm, dignity and intelligence.

TEMPERAMENT Even-tempered, happy and lively disposition.

HEAD AND SKULL Head large, round, not apple-headed, with no indentation of skull. Muzzle short, blunt, square, not upfaced. Wrinkles clearly defined.

EYES Dark, very large, globular in shape, soft and solicitous in expression, very lustrous, and when excited, full of fire.

EARS Thin, small, soft like black velvet. Two kinds: 'Rose ear' – small drop-ear which folds over and back to reveal the burr; 'Button ear' – ear flap folding forward, tip lying close to skull to cover opening. Preference given to latter.

MOUTH Slightly undershot. Wry mouth, teeth or tongue showing all highly undesirable. Wide lower jaw with incisors almost in a straight line.

NECK Slightly arched to resemble a crest, strong, thick with enough length to carry head proudly.

FOREQUARTERS Legs very strong, straight, of moderate length, and well under body. Shoulders well sloped.

BODY Short and cobby, wide in chest and well ribbed. Topline level neither roached nor dipping.

HINDQUARTERS Legs very strong, of moderate length, with good turn of stifle, well under body, straight and parallel when viewed from rear.

FEET Neither so long as the foot of a hare, nor so round as that of the cat; well split up toes; the nails black.

TAIL (Twist) High-set, curled as tightly as possible over hip. Double curl highly desirable.

GAIT/MOVEMENT Viewed from in front should rise and fall with legs well under shoulder, feet keeping directly to front, not turning in or out. From behind, action just as true. Using forelegs strongly, putting them well forward with hindlegs moving freely and using stifles well. A slight roll of hindquarters typifies gait.

COAT Fine, smooth, soft, short and glossy, neither harsh nor woolly.

COLOUR Silver, apricot, fawn or black. Each clearly defined, to make contrast complete between colour, trace (black line extending from occiput to twist) and mask. Markings clearly defined. Muzzle or mask, ears, moles on cheeks, thumb mark or diamond on forehead and trace as black as possible.

IDEAL WEIGHT 6.3-8.1 kgs (14-18 lbs).

FAULTS Any departure from the foregoing points should be considered a fault and the seriousness with which the fault should be regarded should be in exact proportion to its degree.

NOTE Male animals should have two apparently normal testicles fully descended into the scrotum.

Reproduced by kind permission of the English Kennel Club.

THE AMERICAN BREED STANDARD

GENERAL APPEARANCE Symmetry and general appearance are decidedly square and cobby. A lean, leggy Pug and a dog with short legs and a long body are equally objectionable.

SIZE, PROPORTION, SUBSTANCE The Pug should be multum in parvo, and this condensation (if the word may be used) is shown by compactness of form, well knit proportions, and hardness of developed muscle. Weight from 14 to 18 pounds (dog or bitch) desirable. Proportion square.

HEAD The head is large, massive, round – not apple-headed, with no indentation of the skull. The eyes are dark in color, very large, bold and prominent, globular in shape, soft and solicitous in expression, very lustrous, and, when excited, full of fire. The ears are thin, small, soft, like black velvet. There are two kinds – the "rose" and the "button". Preference is given to the latter. The wrinkles are large and deep. The muzzle is short, blunt, square, but

Points of the Pug,
illustrated by Ch. Maulick Upsy-Daisy.
BoB Crufts 1996. Owner/breeder Monica
Hopkinson.   *Photo: Russell Fine Art.*

1. Skull	*9. Shoulder*	*17. Buttock*
2. Lips	*10. Point of Elbow*	*18. Twist*
3. Underjaw	*11. Hock(point)*	*19. Loin*
4. Throat	*12. Flank*	*20. Back*
5. Arm	*13. Stifle joint*	*21. Withers*
6. Wrist	*14. Toes (hind)*	*22. Ear*
7. Brisket	*15. Hock*	*23. Nose and Stop*
8. Toes (front)	*16. Thigh*	

not upfaced. Bite – a Pug's bite should be very slightly undershot.

NECK, TOPLINE, BODY The neck is slightly arched. It is strong, thick, and with enough length to carry the head proudly. The short back is level from the withers to the high tail set. The body is short and cobby, wide in chest and well ribbed up. The tail is curled as tightly as possible over the hip. The double curl is perfection.

FOREQUARTERS The legs are very strong, straight, of moderate length, and are set well under. The elbows should be directly under the withers when viewed from the side. The shoulders are moderately laid back. The pasterns are strong, neither steep nor down. the feet are neither so long as the foot of the hare, nor so round as that of the cat; well split-up toes, and the nails black. Dewclaws are generally removed.

HINDQUARTERS The strong, powerful hindquarters have moderate bend of stifle and short hocks perpendicular to the ground. The legs are parallel when viewed from behind. The hindquarters are in balance with the forequarters. The thighs and buttocks are full and muscular. Feet as in front.

COAT The colors are silver, apricot-fawn, or black. The silver or apricot-fawn colors should be decided so as to make the contrast complete between the color and the trace and the mask.

MARKINGS The markings are clearly defined. The muzzle or mask, ears, moles on cheeks, thumb mark or diamond on forehead, and the back trace should be as black as possible. The mask should be black. The more intense and well defined it is, the better. The trace is a black line extending from the occiput to the tail.

GAIT Viewed from the front, the forelegs should be carried well forward, showing no weakness in the pasterns, the paws landing squarely with the central toes straight ahead. The rear action should be strong and free through hocks and stifles, with no twisting or turning in or out at the joints. The hind legs should follow in line with the front. There is a slight natural convergence of the limbs both fore and aft. A slight roll of the hindquarters typifies the gait which should be free, self-assured, and jaunty.

TEMPERAMENT This is an even-tempered breed, exhibiting stability, playfulness, great charm, dignity, and an outgoing, loving disposition.

Reproduced by kind permission of the American Kennel Club.

THE RIGHTS AND WRONGS
The Breed Standard for the Pug in America is fundamentally the same as that for the UK but, in recent years, a little more explanation has been added to the American Standard. In Britain Pugs are not trimmed, but just kept well-groomed and clean. In America, however, Pugs are prepared for the show ring – all loose hairs are trimmed away from the hind legs and whiskers are removed, even the two little hairs from the beauty spots on the Pug's cheeks.

GENERAL APPEARANCE

For general appearance a Pug should be a square and cobby dog with head and body nicely balanced. A Pug is always described by the Latin term 'multum in parvo' – much in little – and no description could be better than this, for a Pug may be little in size but there is plenty in the small space. How this little dog is put together is essential. To be concerned with just one part of the Pug, such as a beautiful head or the remarkable personality is not quite the thing. The Pug must have balance, good temperament, everything in proportion and, most of all, soundness.

HEAD

The head is large, round and flat on top between the ears. The size of the head must be in proportion to the body. Since the Standard states "head large", sometimes too much emphasis is put on the large head in comparison with the size of the body. Also one can often see a lovely, square, compact body with the head too small and sunk into the shoulders. Neither of these make a balanced Pug. The wrinkles on the forehead should be plentiful and have good

Incorrect: Apple-head and flying ears.

pigmentation so that the lines show distinctly. Strange but true, no two Pugs have the same wrinkles. A dark thumb-mark or diamond in the centre of the forehead is an added beauty.

EYES

The Pug's eyes should be large and globular, expressive, full of fire and with a look of intelligence. A Pug talks with its eyes which are one of its most attractive features. These beautiful eyes must be dark. Light eyes are a serious fault; small eyes are most undesirable. Lots of care must be taken of a Pug's eyes for they can easily be damaged. Waste no time if your Pug hurts an eye. Seek veterinary advice at once. Quick attention is beneficial for quick healing.

EARS

Two kinds of ears are permitted. The 'rose ear', which folds closely to the head, and the 'Button ear', which forms a neat triangle. The tip of the ear should be level with the eyes. The ears must be black and soft as velvet. At no time should the inside of the ears be seen, this is a fault; so are extra large ears, those that are not jet black

Correct head, with large, globular eyes.

Rose ears.

Button ears.

maintain a 'Button ear'. This is done especially at the time of teething, when they are inclined to fly.

MASK
The whole mask must be black. The nose is dark and flat to the face, with large nostrils. It is framed by an over-nose wrinkle and care should be taken of the flesh inside that wrinkle as it could become sore. A little Vaseline will help, then wipe clean, very gently, and powder. On either side of the mask, the cheeks should be well-cushioned, with a black beauty spot on each side with two little black hairs emerging. Some Pugs have a double beauty spot.

Incorrect: Plain head, showing nose.

and ears that fly. The Standard states that preference should be given to the 'Button ears', but in the UK either are accepted. During the 1960s, 1970s and 1980s, rose ears were greatly admired because they looked so much smaller and neater. It certainly did not make any difference when it came to awarding prizes. I have personally had Champions with button or rose ears. However, in America and some other countries they do prefer the 'Button ear'. One very seldom sees a picture of an American Pug with rose ears. I have a number of American books on the Pug but rarely have any of the prize-winning Pugs displayed rose ears. These days many breeders will fix the ear in position with tape when the puppy is young so as to

JAW
A Pug's jaw should be broad. If narrow, there will be drooping lips and the chin will be hidden, which gives a mournful expression. A crooked jaw, refereed to as a wry mouth, causes the tongue to show, which is most undesirable and a serious fault. The Standard states that the bite should be slightly undershot. The word 'slightly' was an adjustment to the Breed Standard a few years ago. I personally was

*Incorrect: Wry mouth,
showing tongue.*

*Incorrect: Too much
lip and narrow jaw.*

use of the strength in their necks. When you place your hand on the crest of the neck, your Pug will push backwards against your hand, raise its legs from the ground and elevate itself to the comfort of your lap. This is one of the most endearing characteristics of the Pug and, as far as I know, no other breed of dog does it.

FOREQUARTERS
The forequarters of a Pug should be positive, by which is meant there should be a good, deep, fairly wide chest with amply-boned straight legs. The pasterns should be strong, not weak, or the feet will turn outwards in an exaggerated position. Forelegs out at the elbows, or Chippendale, and weak pasterns are all faults. The shoulders should be laid back, nicely sloped.

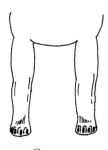

Correct.

*Incorrect:
Narrow front.*

not in favour of this as I felt it would be misused, so it is something that one must be careful about. If the bite is too much undershot the teeth will show when the mouth is closed and this is a fault. The teeth should be in straight alignment.

NECK
A Pug should have a strong neck on good shoulders with a slight arch, called the crest, at the back of the skull. This will enable the head to be carried correctly. Too many Pugs today have heads that are sunk into the shoulders. Pugs can make good

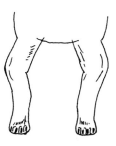

*Incorrect: Forelegs
out at the elbows.*

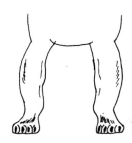

*Incorrect: Forelegs
Queen Anne or
Chippendale.*

BODY

Sideways-on the body should look quite square, with a good level topline. To dip on the shoulders is wrong, so is a roached back. A Pug requires a good rib cage and a firm solid frame. Too short coupled or a long body is a fault, as it takes away the squareness that is required.

HINDQUARTERS

When viewing the hindquarters from behind, the legs must be straight, not cow-hocked (turning out) or bow-legged (turning in). From the side view one should see a good turn of stifle, not straight or light-boned. The thigh should be nicely muscled. Weak hindquarters will cause the dog to limp. This could be a sign of either hip dysplasia or slipping patella, both of which are hereditary.

Correct: Good level topline.

Incorrect: Dip on shoulders, long body.

Incorrect: No neck and low set tail.

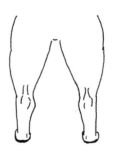

Correct.

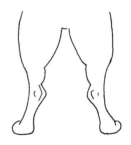

Incorrect: Cow-hocked.

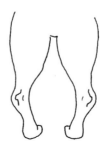

Incorrect: Bow-legged.

Correct:
Good turn of stifle.

Incorrect:
Straight stiffle.

FEET

Feet should be neat in appearance. They should not spread out with toes long and separated like those of a hare. A Pug should not be flat-footed but should stand on the pad with the short toes slightly arched. Toenails must be black. They should be kept short, preferably through exercise. Walking on hard ground acts like an emery board on the nails and keeps them short. If necessary a Pug's toenails can be clipped, but we all know how a Pug hates this. Dewclaws are often removed when puppies are a few days old. If they are not, they must be kept short, otherwise the nails grow and can curl back into the flesh.

Correct feet.

Incorrect:
Spread feet.

TAIL

The tail must be set high, not standing high, the twist lying flat over the back. This gives the appearance of a little bottom. A double twist is most desirable, but the length is not the be all and end all, providing the tail is curled round and not too short, loose or low-set. It makes no difference which side the twist curls. At one stage in the late eighteenth century it was thought that the curl of the tail lay one side for a dog and the other for a bitch, but this has proved to be an old wives' tale.

GAIT

The gait of the Pug should be exactly as the Standard states. The movement is a rhythmic two-beat diagonal gait in which the feet at diagonally opposite ends of the body strike the ground together. It is incorrect for a Pug to pace. The slight roll should not be confused with gait. It comes from the hindquarters and not the criss-crossing of back legs. I like to refer to the back movement as being similar to a top fashion model on the cat walk. The legs move straight and even, but the hips sway from side to side. The correct movement of a Pug is, indeed, a joy to watch.

COAT

The Breed Standard gives a good description of the texture of a Pug's coat. I cannot improve on this. Of course it does need to be kept well brushed to remove loose hairs and to be given the occasional bath. I don't believe in too many baths, which may remove the natural, protective oil from the coat, but this is only a personal opinion.

COLOUR

The colour silver is like cold stone with

silver hairs. It is very seldom seen these days. Apricot, often now termed apricot-fawn, is a light fawn with a rich apricot saddle. There are all shades of fawn from dark to light. The dark fawn coat must not be too dark or become smutty in appearance. Some coats are getting too light, more cream than fawn. Breeders must watch this carefully or they will lose the dark points of the Pug. All these colours should carry a trace, a black line down the centre of the back. Most puppies, when they are born, do show this deep black line but, as they mature, this tends to spread into a saddle. All Pugs should carry some indication of that dark line. Always remember the three important points of the Pug that must be black – the ears, mask and toenails; and we must not forget those lovely, dark eyes.

The coat of a black Pug must be shining jet black, no white, rust or brown hairs and once again those lovely, dark eyes must be evident. As there is no contrast in the colour of the black it is very difficult to define the wrinkle. It is therefore important that a black Pug's wrinkles should be deep.

WEIGHT

The Standards state that the weight of a Pug is 14-18 lbs (6.3-8.1 kgs). Today very few are seen at 14 lbs. Do not be deceived by the look. Pugs should have good bone and this adds weight which is very deceiving to the eye when comparing size. Although we do like to see the nice-sized Pug weighing around 18 lbs, there are still far too many large Pugs reaching over 20 lbs. On the other hand, by breeding to size we do not want to lose the bone; a Pug must have good, solid bone. These are all points to be watched.

THE POINT SYSTEM

As a guideline to identifying the qualities of a Pug, the following point system was established by the Pug Dog Club in 1893 and it hasn't been changed since. This shows the relative importance of each aspect of a Pug's conformation.

	Fawn	Black
Symmetry	10	10
Size	5	10
Condition	5	5
Body	10	10
Legs and feet	5	5
Head	5	5
Muzzle	10	10
Ears	5	5
Eyes	5	5
Mask	5	-
Wrinkles	10	10
Tail	10	10
Trace	5	-
Coat	5	5
Colour	5	10
Total	100	100

SUMMARY

Going through the Standard I have tried to give, in as much detail as I can, the important points to watch for. If I have emphasised different points of the Pug as being important, that does not mean that you should be dismayed if any of these wrongs apply to your own Pug. There is no perfect Pug – that is the aim of breeding. Just consider your Pug's virtues and not your Pug's peculiarities.

7 *BREEDING*

Having fallen for the Pug, you have now decided you would like to breed from your bitch. You must of course have looked around, observed her wonderful character and become familiar with the many ways of caring for this delightful breed. But it may not be as easy as you think. Breeding involves a lot of hard work, care, disappointments and some heartbreaks, and it is very time-consuming. It is a responsibility that will demand your whole attention. First and foremost you must make sure your bitch has all the right qualities for breeding. She should be strongly built, active and hard in muscular condition, and free from any deformities. If you bought her from a well-established breeder, they will help you with knowledge and experience and be able to answer many questions. Bitches have a season approximately every six months, usually starting from the age of seven to nine months. The ideal time to start breeding would be on the second or third season, when your bitch would be between 18 months to two years. Never breed on two consecutive seasons and certainly not after she reaches six years of age. This complies with the Pug Dog Club code of ethics.

CHOOSING A SIRE

Prior to mating your bitch you will have had time to look around at other Pugs and will be aware your own Pug's faults. You will also have had the chance to see the kind of Pug you would like to breed. Take note of the puppies and young adults at the dog shows. See how they are bred. If a certain dog is producing puppies of quality which could fill your need, he will be the one worth considering.

When choosing a sire, first ask to see his pedigree and be sure that it does not contain the name of a dog or bitch that has any hereditary defects of which you are aware. Should this occur, then you must be very careful that this name is not also on your bitch's pedigree; never double in trouble. Talk this over with the breeder of your bitch, especially if you wish to line breed. Line breeding is when you mate your bitch back to the second or third generation, that is, to a grandparent or before. Sometimes it is necessary to go to a complete outcross, that is a dog whose pedigree is completely different from that of your bitch. This is something that you will learn over the years but, as a newcomer, it is best to consult someone with experience on the matter, probably the owner of the sire that you are considering using. I am sure they will help you in your final decision. Now you are still looking for the right sire, one that will be the most compatible with your bitch. Study everything carefully. Try to choose a sire that excels in the qualities that your bitch lacks. Do not make mistakes by going to the stud dog living nearest, just for the sake of convenience. Also, do not use a certain dog because he is producing large litters. The sire has nothing to do with the number of puppies born in the litter. It is quality you want, not quantity. The same thing applies to Champions – not all are successful stud dogs. It is not advisable to mate a maiden bitch with an untried dog.

MATING FOR A TRUE BLACK PUG

As regards mating a black bitch, this has always been a delicate subject. Breeders of blacks seem to have their own ideas. Some insist on mating black to black. Others feel that a fawn can be introduced successfully, and it has been proved so in the past. To expand on the subject, I quote from a hand-written letter that is in the Pug Dog Club Historian archives, in which the late Mrs V. A. Graham, the breeder of Edenderry Pugs for over fifty years wrote: "I have been asked repeatedly to write an article on black breeding. This is a subject I don't really want to get involved with in case I hurt anyone's feelings. These are my own experiences on black breeding for what they are worth. I have always stuck to my idea of Black to Black. I have never found this method of breeding wrong in the end product, providing the dam and the sire are assured of receiving the correct minerals in their diet. This is most important, I feel sure, in any breed where

one hopes to get the correct pigmentation. It is essential in both fawns and blacks alike that they are given the right trace elements.

"I have only crossed blacks and fawns as far as I can remember three or four times since I started to breed Pugs in 1922. I mated (pure Black) Edenderry Allanagh, litter sister of Ch. Edenderry Banshee, to Springs Herald of Broadway (clear Fawn) in 1935. This mating produced Ch. Edenderry Cuan, who was one of the youngest English Champions ever. He was good-coloured black, although there were two fawns, not a good colour, from this mating. Cuan was eventually mated to a pure black-bred bitch, Edenderry Dierdre. She had a litter of four black. The pick of this litter, Edenderry Annie Rooney, a very lovely bitch, was, in turn, mated to a good black dog. The offspring from this litter was disappointing regarding colour. They were not a good black, which proves the theory I have always gone by that, when breeding, it is more essential to know the colours and qualities and faults of the grandparents and great grandparents than of the parents. I have done this fawn and black mating once since and the results have only been fair.

"If I am asked by a breeder who is really and truly interested in results I give them my advice for what it is worth. I would never try to influence anyone wishing to try crossing the colours but I have never found it to be of any advantage. If black is mated to black, with particular attention paid to correct trace elements or minerals, and the bitch fed on good raw meat while carrying her puppies, the result can only be black."

All this consideration in finding the right mate for your bitch, whether black or fawn, is to produce the ideal Pug, one that has all the good qualities of this lovely breed.

PREPARING FOR THE MATING

Your bitch should be wormed regularly. If she has not been so treated, make sure she is wormed a month or so before her season is due. Also, make sure that she has had her yearly booster. By now you will have already made arrangements with the owners of the sire. Warn them immediately your bitch comes into season. The first day of the season is when the bitch begins to show colour. Once the season starts, keep your bitch away from all other dogs, especially strange ones, but she can still have the company of her female companions at home. I must repeat that one must be very careful when taking a bitch out for a walk and I cannot emphasise enough that I would certainly never let a child take a bitch in season for a walk. It is far too risky for the child and the bitch. Personally, when my bitches are in season, and especially when I am about to mate one, I try to keep away from public places where other dogs have been, in order to avoid any infectious diseases and germs.

The time for mating is about the 12th to 14th day of the season, but this is just a guide. Often the owner of the sire will ask for the dog and bitch to meet on one of these days. Keep your eye on your bitch, notice when the colour begins to cease. If you tickle the lower end of her spine, her tail may move in an unusual way. She will begin to play up to her companions. All this is will give you some idea that she is ready to meet her mate. The right time for mating is when the bitch will stand and is willing to accept the dog, and this can vary any time from the 10th to 20th day, sometimes before, or sometimes later.

I well remember one peaceful Sunday morning, when the dinner was in the oven, all set for my husband Arthur and me to have our Sunday meal. Pyramida, much to my surprise, decided to show all the signs that she was ready for mating, this being the tenth day of her season. I rang Audrey Gibson, the owner of the dog that I was going to use. "Bring her at once," she said. We turned out the oven and off we set, a journey of about eighty miles ahead of us. When we arrived, the dog was introduced to the bitch, but neither were interested. Audrey said, "Let's have lunch and try again afterwards." Again, no success. Audrey suggested that we left Pyramida, as probably she wasn't quite ready. Arthur and I made our way home. We had just got in the front door when the telephone rang. It was Audrey. "Success, Ellen, a good mating," she exclaimed. Pyramida stayed with the Gibsons for two days for a repeat mating. The result was four lovely puppies.

It is more usual to take the bitch to the dog. Obviously, one cannot keep travelling day after day waiting for the right moment. The owner of the sire may suggest keeping your bitch until she has been mated. This can be done at your own discretion. The owner may also suggest a second mating two days later but this is not always the case.

THE MATING

The important day has arrived. All decisions have been made and you are now on your way to mate your bitch. Do make sure not to feed her before your journey and that she has relieved herself before meeting her mate. If possible, it is better to be with your bitch at the time of mating, so she has the confidence of your presence. It must be most upsetting for her to be put into a stranger's hands, go to a stranger's home and be left to be mated, not knowing what is happening, especially if she is a maiden bitch. In some cases she could resist and worry the sire. On the other hand, the owner of the sire may prefer you not to be in the room at the time of mating; she will understand the temperament of her dog. This is something you will decide between yourselves.

The usual satisfactory mating is a tie which can last 10 to 40 minutes. After the mating, let your bitch rest comfortably alone. It is better not to let her relieve herself for an hour or so. However, never be dismayed if there is no tie. A bitch has often conceived without. I know from my own experience that this can happen. Catherina, my bitch, was ready to be mated when Arthur and I arrived at Susan Graham-Weall's home. She was introduced to the dog but, try as we may, there was no success. The bitch didn't like the dog and the dog didn't like the bitch. Susan suggested that we had lunch and tried again afterwards. Still no success. We had given up hope. Before getting into the car for our homeward journey, Arthur took Catherina for a walk to relieve herself. On the way back Arthur was waving something in the air saying, "I've always looked for one of these and never been successful." It turned out to be a four-leafed clover. No charge was made for the mating as there had been no tie and we were all disappointed. However, much to our surprise, nine weeks later, four lovely puppies arrived. So it can happen. I thought of the song, "I'm looking over a four-leafed clover....there was one for the sunshine, one for the rain and one for the roses that bloom in the lane, there's no need explaining the one remaining..." So my surviving puppies were named after the four-leafed clover: Goodchance Rainsparkle, Rosalia and Radiant Sun.

Settle your agreements with the owner of the sire before leaving. There may be papers to be signed, fees to be paid and arrangements as regards puppies. Do make sure this is done in a professional manner and proper agreements are signed by both parties. You would be surprised how often in the heat of the moment things are misunderstood and cause problems at a later date. Now comes the waiting time.

THE BITCH IN WHELP

For the first few weeks after mating life for the bitch goes on as normal. Keep a watchful eye about the 28th day. Note whether the nipples are getting pink and look for a clear mucous discharge from the vulva. This is usually a good sign that the bitch has conceived. At this stage you could visit your vet, who will give you a satisfactory result one way or the other. If you have good news, then from now on you have the care of your mother-to-be. Gradually increase her diet. If she has been used to one meal a day, now make it into two, adding a little more each time but cutting down on biscuits. Then by the last two weeks, divide the food into three or four meals, as this will avoid her having any discomfort. Also add calcium to the diet and, maybe, yeast tablets and halibut oil each day. A bitch must have sufficient calcium to avoid the trouble of eclampsia. Fortunately we very seldom hear of it in Pugs. During the last week, half a teaspoon of Milk of Magnesia daily is most useful for controlling the digestive system. At all times keep fresh clean water available; a little glucose can be added. During pregnancy your bitch can lead a normal life. Take her for a walk but don't overdo it. Above all try to avoid her jumping on chairs or running up stairs. It is better to be safe than sorry! Make sure you have everything prepared and ready for the delivery. The whelping box, which is about 2ft (60cm) square and 2ft high, should be placed in a warm, quiet corner of the room. It should be clean and comfortable. A bar attached about 4 inches (10cm) from the floor and 3 inches (7.5cm) from the inside wall of the box is very useful, as Pugs can be very careless with their puppies. If one of the litter crawls round the back of the mother, it is so easy for her unknowingly to lie on that puppy. The bar will prevent this. Whelping boxes of this description can be bought from any reputable dealer. I would advise that the best place to purchase one is at a Championship Dog Show.

Allow the mother-to-be to sleep in the whelping box for the last two weeks of her pregnancy. This will get her used to her new bed. Give her plenty of old cloths, anything that she can scratch and tear, as she prepares her 'nest' for her new arrivals. All breeders have their own method of how to keep the bed clean and tidy for their puppies. I always have two hard boards cut to the size of the whelping box floor. The hard board I cover with layers of newspaper, then cover with flannelette sheeting and fix underneath. The bed is then flat, with no wrinkles or lumps for discomfort. This board slides neatly into the whelping box. The second board is covered exactly the same and stands by ready to be exchanged when the bed is dirty. In this way the bed is always kept clean and is changed quickly. These days, breeders find synthetic bedding most convenient, but whatever you use, keep the bed nice and clean and warm.

Puppies must be kept warm. You may use an infra-red lamp hung from above, an electric blanket or a hot water bottle but, whatever you choose, never ever lose the heat. I always use an infra-ray lamp hung from above and this can be raised or lowered according to the need. I did, on one occasion, use an electric blanket and found it very useful when the puppies were very young. As they grew older and were getting a little mischievous I was afraid of the electric wires.

Other things you will need at hand are:-
A small cardboard box to fit a covered hot water bottle.
Sheeting to cover over the cardboard box.
Pieces of soft towelling to grip puppies at birth.
A pair of scissors to cut the umbilical cord.
A small bowl of disinfectant to keep the scissors in.
Strong thread for tying puppies' umbilical cords.
A bowl of disinfectant to wash your own hands and a clean towel to dry them.
Plenty of newspaper.
Weighing scales.
A bucket for afterbirths.

It is always worthwhile to let your vet know when you have puppies due, as one never knows if he will be needed in the case of an emergency, especially if it should happen during a night delivery.

THE BIRTH
Gestation is sixty-two to sixty-three days, but whelping may occur any time from the fifty-eighth day. It is advisable if nothing happens by the sixty-sixth day to consult your vet. Most bitches will refuse food sometime before whelping. The mother-to-be will lie quiet for a while, then start to scratch in corners, tearing up paper and any soft materials around. Soon she will begin to pant and turn around as labour pains increase and become more frequent. She

Choisya Chocy Chip in her 61st day of gestation. Owned by Alison Su.

will be quite restless. Do not worry her – nature will take its course. Sometimes a bitch will want to run around, a little panicky when the puppies are ready to be born. If this does happen, hold her gently and firmly with words of comfort.

Keep with your bitch constantly at this stage, for as soon as a puppy is born, your immediate attention will be required. Because Pugs have flat faces it is difficult for them to deal with the membrane (amniotic sac) and umbilical cord, so this is where your work will begin. Once the puppies are born the afterbirth will follow attached to the umbilical cord. If it doesn't, hold puppy with a piece of soft towelling and gently pull the afterbirth out. Try not to let it break. Cut the membrane under the chin and pull it over the head and body. Clear the face and nostrils of any fluid. Tie the cord about one inch from the puppy's abdomen. It is said that it is the natural thing for bitches to eat the afterbirth. I know some people do let their bitches have just one. Personally I would never let my Pugs do this. I dispose of the afterbirth

immediately, but I do make sure to count them so nothing is left behind when whelping is finished.

These last paragraphs are, as one might say, "according to the book", but there are times when difficulties arise, such as breech births (when legs arrive first) and afterbirths left behind. Don't be too disturbed about the latter as it will no doubt arrive with the next puppy, but do make sure you have the same number of afterbirths as puppies. Problems like these are not anything to worry about unduly, but to anyone who has not experienced them before they can be quite perturbing. As a beginner it really would be helpful to have with you an experienced friend, as you could become a little over-anxious, whereas the friend would be of comfort and would know if at any stage a vet was needed.

The time between puppies varies considerably. Some come, as the saying goes, "like shelling peas". Others take their time. One can expect roughly between 30 to 45 minutes between puppies. If, however, it reaches two hours and, especially if the bitch appears uncomfortable by bearing down and nothing happening, then maybe it would be necessary to consult the vet, because a simple injection of synthetic oxytocin will help.

Wrap the puppy in a clean towel and dry thoroughly. Puppy should by now show signs of life. Keep rubbing and moving until the puppy begins to cry (what a joy that is!). This should all be worked confidently and quickly. Pug puppies when born are dark grey, almost black. They have pink noses and pink toes. The face is flat, with tiny ears that lie upwards flat to the head. The tail hangs loose. There is no mistake in their breed. They look like Pugs from the start. Should there be any difficulty in bringing life, keep the puppy moving to get the circulation going. Try breathing into the mouth; swing up and down – high and low; lay puppy on its back, moving the forelegs. Never give up – some puppies take longer than others to show life. Keep persevering; only give up when you are sure there is no hope.

Breeder Jean Manifold had one of the strangest experiences – the veterinary surgeon said that the eight-week-old puppy was alive because of a million-to-one chance. When the puppy was born, Jean noticed that it was weaker than the rest of the litter. Despite all efforts it grew even weaker and Jean was not surprised when its little heart stopped. She telephoned the vet for a post-mortem in case the puppy had a disease that might have affected the other puppies. On the vet's advice the puppy was wrapped in newspaper put in a polythene bag and placed in the fridge to keep it fresh. Five hours later the vet called at Jean's home. Afterwards, the vet said, "I was just about to cut the puppy open when I thought I saw its mouth twitch. I realised it wasn't dead. Mrs Manifold and myself bathed the pup in hot water and heated it over a cooker ring. Slowly it thawed out. The puppy couldn't have been dead when it was put in the fridge, although its heart had stopped beating. If the dog hadn't been wrapped it would have died because of the intense cold. As it was, there was just enough air in the polythene bag for the puppy to breath. The puppy was frozen stiff – but not to the point of death." This puppy grew to maturity and spent a long and happy life.

THE NURSING MOTHER

After giving birth, the mother will no doubt have gone back to bed and settled down. Having got the puppy dry and breathing, give the new arrival to mother. She may not want anything to do with it at first. I remember a bitch of mine looking at her first-born in a quite bewildered manner, and barking at him when he moved, and she certainly could not understand what was happening when he cried. Don't worry. Some Pugs take to their babies quicker than others. Lie the new-born puppy in the already prepared warm puppy box and cover with sheeting. Puppies must be kept warm and free from draughts. When the mother feels another puppy due, she will get up and move around. You can try giving her a little warm milk during rest time, but don't worry or fuss her. Soon another puppy will arrive and you will start all over again.

The number of puppies varies considerably. It can be from two to eight, occasionally one hears of more. When you feel the litter has been completed, you may take the bitch out to relieve herself, but have someone to go along with her. While

Choisya Chocy Chip contentedly feeding her six puppies.

she is away the whelping box can be cleaned and tidied up for mother to return to her babies. Wipe the mother clean, especially around the nipples, and see her peacefully settled down and babies suckling. If there are any difficulties with any puppy, gently open the puppy's mouth and insert the nipple, soothing the mother at the same time. It is surprising how quickly a puppy will learn what to do.

Provided everything goes along satisfactorily, you can give your vet a call with the news and, if you have decided to have the puppies' dewclaws removed, arrangements can be made. Having dewclaws removed is not essential. They have no useful purpose but they can be dangerous to Pugs' eyes, not only their own, but also to their brothers and sisters while playing. If they are left on, and then in later life they cause trouble, it is not a particularly easy operation to remove them at that stage.

After the puppies are born, it is advisable to stay with mother and babies day and night for the first few weeks so as to be

there if they need you. One puppy I had was very poorly. She was 6oz at birth but down to 3oz within two days. I drip-fed her every two hours, day and night, with very little hope of her surviving. However, while there is life there is hope, so the drip-feeding went on for a further week. Puppy was very limp and still only 3oz. "She will never live," I said. I think she must have heard, for suddenly the scale moved half-an-ounce on and continued to do so. From then on drip-feeding became a little less, as I would now hold her on to her mother. I was winning. I could see her growing, only half the size of her brothers and sister but now quite active. So Rosa, my miracle baby, lived on to go in the show ring – not a Champion, but quite successful. She at least got her name in the Stud Book and is an absolute joy of a Pug to own.

Sometimes it does become necessary to drip-feed a puppy as I did with Rosa. I used a syringe containing a well-known puppy milk and fed her with just a few drips at a time. I do know breeders who, very successfully, use yoghurt bio-active extra mild, fed at room temperature.

For the first few days mother should only be given liquid food, such as warm milk and egg mixture. Later one can introduce white meat and fish in small quantities, three or four times a day. At the end of the first week, red meat can be added to the diet. Calcium, halibut oil and vitamin should be given to mother daily while she is nursing. After a week, mother can go back to normal, good, healthy feeding – but do make sure she has plenty of liquid. Mother deals with all the puppies' toilet arrangements during the early days. Should you feel that there are any constipation problems, simply massage gently with baby oil. This is something worth watching.

It is courteous to let the owner of the sire know when the bitch begins to whelp. Being interested in the well-being of your bitch and her offspring, this owner may even ask to be contacted continuously throughout the deliveries. Then for the next two weeks you should be able to see a happy and contented family.

REARING THE LITTER
The rearing of a litter of puppies is the most important duty of a breeder. The start that these small animals have in life plays an influential part in their future. We often hear people say "Mrs So-and-So always comes out with a good puppy" or "Mrs What's-her Name is lucky, she has another nice puppy to show. That will soon be a Champion." The reason that Mrs So-and-So and Mrs What's-her-Name always have a good puppy to show is because they have learnt how to breed and rear their puppies properly. Doing this job correctly is time-consuming and hard work. Keeping puppies clean, and fed with a correct diet and trained into strong healthy Pugs does

credit to the breeders, and their reward is seen in the show ring. Not all puppies go into the show ring; some are sold as pets to good homes, and their owners return, again and again, to the same breeder when they sadly lose their much-loved pet. Such breeders have earned themselves a worthy reputation for good stock.

In this chapter I am not telling you what you should do – every breeder has their own ideas and would probably object to being told. We all learn by reading and talking to other breeders and, when the time comes to put this into practice, you will find that each litter you have is different in some way and there is always some story to tell. We are still learning what is best. I shall just tell you what I do. You may agree or disagree – that is beside the point, but I hope something is learnt by it.

THE FIRST THREE WEEKS
I always keep a puppy diary. I start this from the time my bitch first comes into season and write an account of every day's happenings, right until my last puppy goes to his or her new owner. You will be surprised how useful this is. I also make a weight chart for the puppies. Each puppy is first weighed every other day until one month old, then weighed once a week.

So, having got your lovely litter of puppies settled down with mother, you should have quite a peaceful three weeks. Between the tenth and fifteenth day you will notice their eyes beginning to open. At this stage I usually pull the curtains and keep the nest in semi-darkness. The bright light is not good when the eyes first open. You will now notice that their toenails are getting very sharp, which hurt the mother. Just take the tips off with sharp nail clippers and continue doing this as often as is necessary.

FEEDING

At the end of the third week teeth will begin to appear, and this is when supplementary feeding can start. I buy the best of beef and scrape it to a pulp with the back of a knife. Each puppy is given a piece of the raw meat the size of a marble. I lie a large pillow on a table and let the puppy nestle into it. I like feeding my young puppies on the table, rather than on my lap, as I think it is more secure and it gets a puppy used to the table right from the start. I talk continuously, and let the puppy get well settled, before offering the meat. Some will take to it right away, others will keep having it in and out of the mouth before swallowing it. The puppy will have this small taste of meat again the next day. On the third day I introduce a cereal. One dessertspoon of simulated bitch's milk, to one teaspoon of baby cereal, and a quarter of a teaspoon of honey is sufficient for three puppies. Later in the day the puppies have their raw meat.

At this stage, which is about the twenty-fifth day, your puppies should be walking about with their tails up, playing with each other and enjoying these small meals. It is necessary now to have a reasonably spacious pen so that the puppies can have a good area in which to run around. This is also the time to train your puppies to be clean.

A drink of milk formula (of your own choice) can be introduced to each day's diet. What milk you use is important. One puppy I had suddenly developed a dreadful staring coat, where the hair was standing up and the flesh was quite pink. My vet took the puppy in for a week, trying to find out what was wrong, only to discover it was the puppy milk. He was allergic to any supplementary milk whatsoever. From then on it was water only, and rice made with water also. None of the other puppies in the litter were affected. Incidentally, he grew out of this allergy later on.

By the time the puppies are four weeks old they should be having four meals a day: cereal at breakfast; milk drink at lunch time; meat in the evening; and the cereal mixture at night, with one drop of a multi-vitamin supplement, such as Abidec. This will

Weaning is a gradual process, and if done tactfully, the puppies will soon be feeding well.

contain all the necessary vitamins required for rearing puppies. This was recommended to me by my vet twenty-five years ago and I have always used it since, and I have been surprised at the number of times, when attending seminars over the years on different Toy breeds, that it has been mentioned.

When puppies are five weeks old, diet is increased slightly, and they should now be having five meals a day. Let mother give puppies a last feed at night, then she can leave her babies to spend the night alone. By this time she has already been leaving them occasionally during the day. Puppies by now should be happy and contented individuals. Puppy meal with a meat extract gravy is now added to their meat. A day's diet at eight weeks old should be:-

Breakfast: Baby cereal, mixed with milk and a little honey followed by a wholemeal rusk to chew.
Lunch: One dessertspoonful of minced meat with puppy meal mixed with meat extract gravy.

Tea: Milk food mixed with cereal of your choice or baby rice.
Evening Meal: As for lunch. Chicken or fish can be given as an alternative to meat.
Supper: Hard-boiled egg mashed into a trifle sponge cake with a small knob of margarine (about as large as a walnut). This mixture should serve four puppies. Milk to drink.
Daily: One drop of Abidec and calcium according to instructions.
All food should be given at blood heat. Fresh clean water should be available at all times, with maybe a little glucose added.

My puppies are each given their own dish. I do not believe in putting a bowl of food down for all to fend for themselves. Some puppies are slower than others and can miss out on food because of the greedy ones. Never leave food down after a meal. Take all dishes up, hopefully empty. If you do have a puppy who is proving difficult about eating, after the litter brothers and sisters are finished and out exercising, take this puppy alone, who may need a little encouragement to eat properly.

This diet is the basic food requirement

for a healthy Pug puppy, but one cannot say exactly what quantity is needed. It all depends on the appetite and tastes of the individual. Some puppies may require more than others – but do not over-feed. A Pug needs a good, firm body and strong muscle but, if over-fed, the body becomes heavy. This weight could spoil the legs and shoulders because, until the puppy becomes an adult, the bones are just gristle. New dry puppy foods are constantly being brought out onto the market and it is worth seeking more information from manufacturers if you would prefer to feed your puppies in this way.

PUPPIES AT SIX WEEKS

At six weeks puppies should be wormed. It is best to obtain medicine from a vet so that you can be sure it is fresh. The young puppies need plenty of fresh air and exercise, but do this at the right time, one that suits your own convenience, but never after a meal. Put the puppies out after they have eaten a meal to go to the toilet, let them have a little run around, then put them straight back into bed to rest. My Pugs, adults as well as puppies, always rest after a meal. By now the dark puppy hairs have gone and the fawn or apricot is coming through. The Pug trace (a black line down the centre of the back), inherited from their ancestors, is now clearly shown but, unfortunately, it does go as puppies get older leaving a saddle when an adult.

TRAINING

Training starts the moment a puppy is able to leave the mother's nest and crawl out into the surrounding pen. A dirt tray, or just a newspaper placed in a corner, will give the puppies the opportunity to find a clean spot to relieve themselves. It really is surprising how quickly puppies learn to do this. Directly you see the puppy awake and moving about, gently place the puppy on the paper. This also applies after a feed. It is never too young to get into a clean habit. By nature a dog does not like a dirty bed, so will soon understand what that corner of the pen is for. For some while you will have to keep an eye on your puppy's movements. When you notice the puppy starting to whimper, sniff the floor or run around in circles, put that puppy into the place which you want to serve as the relieving area. Wait until the puppy has finished, then give lots of praise. Normally puppies will want to relieve themselves on waking up and after each feed so, immediately out of a sleep and directly a meal is finished, either place the puppy on the dirt tray or newspaper, or outside if the weather is fine.

You will find that, during the teething time, the puppies will go around chewing everything in sight. Give the puppies a few hard rubber toys and tough chew sticks. Providing your puppies are in a good-sized play pen, use will be made of these as there will be nothing else to be destructive with. If, perhaps, the bed itself is chewed, scold with that harsh voice and give one of the toys to play with and, eventually, the idea of chewing the bed will be gone. As a last resort, if the chewing still persists, change the bed to a cardboard box with lots of newspaper in it.

LEAVING HOME

Different breeders have their own ideas about when puppies are ready to go to their new homes. Personally I never let mine go until they have had their inoculations. By then I hope to have trained the puppy to be clean, to be used to walking on the lead and to know how to stand on a table. It is then up to the new owner to continue how I have started. Don't think for one moment that puppy will always carry on from my training. At such a young age a puppy will soon forget. Providing the new owner practises every day what I have started, there will never be any show problems, because the puppy has learnt from the start of life.

Your puppies are now ready to leave you. Do be very careful that you have chosen suitable owners. Tell the new owners all there is to know. Give them a food chart and, if you are like me, plenty of "do's and don'ts" and tell them, if they have any worries at all, to contact you for advice. If your puppy is going to a home where there are children, do warn them that a Pug puppy is not a toy. They must be handled very gently. Pugs love children, so naturally they will enjoy their company, but children should play with them on the floor, so there is no danger of the puppy being dropped and they can play together without any worries.

8 PUGS IN ART

Pug owners are most ardent collectors of Pug memorabilia. No Pug home is complete without a picture hanging on the wall, or a figurine on a shelf or in a showcase. Maybe this is why there is so much interest in Pug antiques and art today. What makes it so fascinating is that the Pug has had a very long existence and some changes in appearance. Many famous artists have used their brushes to portray this delightful and interesting breed of dog. Gathering interesting pictures of art for this book has really left me spellbound. There is so much knowledge to be gained, but

obtaining it has sometimes felt like getting blood out of a stone. I have seen beautiful pictures by famous and not-so-famous artists from 1800 onwards. One such painting is *Playfellows* in oil by Schreiber (1868-1901). The Pug is lying down with children's toys. The doll is lying flat with one foot in the air quite close to the Pug. There is a wide-eyed look of innocence on the Pug's face – it's pretty obvious that he has been having a go at the doll.

There is also *Tick-Tack* (1881), an oil on canvas painting by Briton Riviere (1840-1920). It shows a young Pug, eyes and ears

Richard Boyle, 3rd Earl of Burlington as a boy with his three sisters Elizabeth, Juliana, and Jane (c1700). By Sir Godfrey Kneller.
In the Devonshire Collection, Chatsworth.
Reproduced by permission of the Chatsworth Settlement Trustees.

An Interior with a Lady and Gentleman Seated on a Sofa. By Thomas Patch (1725-1782).
Courtesy: Witt Library, Courtauld Institute of Art.

Arnold Rosenhagen. By Henry Pickering (1738-1771).
Courtesy: Witt Library, Courtauld Institute of Art.

alert and full of curiosity at the sound of a gentleman's fob pocket watch which lies nearby. It is a charming painting which can be seen at the Russell-Coates Art Gallery and Museum in Bournemouth. Another painting which I must mention is *Mischievious Tabbies* by Clemence Meilsson (1879-1911). Two cats are sitting on the table tormenting the Pug who, in desperation to get at them, has dragged the tablecloth, and the contents have fallen to the floor. So typical! In yet another

painting that I have seen and loved, a lady and gentleman are seated on a sofa holding hands. The period looks very much like Regency to me. In one corner of the picture an elderly lady is reading a book, chaperon to the lady on the sofa, no doubt. Peeping through the door is a gentleman. And there lying on the floor, by the seated gentleman's feet, is the wide-eyed Pug, with a corkscrew tail and cropped ears. The artist is Thomas Patch (1725-1782).

In the Devonshire Collection at

Chatsworth House, Derbyshire, there is an intriguing – and large – painting by Sir Godfrey Kneller. It is a portrait of Richard Boyle, 3rd Earl of Burlington, as a child, with three of his six sisters, Elizabeth, Juliana and Jane. It is dated April 25th, 1698. One of the girls is holding a black puppy which has all the features of a Pug. If it was a Pug, as I believe it is, this proves again that black Pugs were in England in the late 17th Century. There are so many artists who have portrayed the Pug, each one showing this little dog in life-like poses. Although the physical appearance may have had its changes, no matter what painting one sees, the character of the Pug has remained. All these paintings may be found in art galleries in the UK.

1400 TO c1760
In about 1400 Albrecht de Vriendt, a Belgian artist, painted a picture of the half-insane King Charles VI of France in which the King was amusing himself with the newly-introduced game of cards. On the left of the picture is a small Greyhound and in the centre sits a Pug dog, typically bedecked with bell on his collar. In 1730 Jean-Baptiste Oudry (1686-1755), a French artist renowned for painting dogs,

painted a picture titled *Pug Dog*. It was a painting of one of Louis XV's favourite dogs and can be seen in the Lille Museum in France. Said to be one of the earliest Pug paintings is *Old Virtue* by Leonard Knyff (1650-1722). To me, his heavy body looks more like a Mastiff than a Pug. However, he has cropped ears, a hanging tongue and the tail looks quite loose. Also he appears to have head wrinkles, so he must be a Pug. Old Virtue's gravestone, dated 1702, can still be seen in the garden at Dunham Massey, near Altrincham, Greater Manchester. Thomas Gainsborough found the Pug a very interesting subject. In the early 1760s he produced a rapidly painted sketch on canvas which depicted the lively characterisation of an alert and intelligent Pug.

HOGARTH (1697-1764)
The artist Hogarth did many paintings of the Pug, the most famous being his self-portrait with Trump, his own Pug, dated 1745. This is an oil on canvas painting which hangs in the Tate Gallery, London. The painting shows all that Hogarth held dear to his heart – the palette for his oils, the books, particularly the works of Shakespeare which he loved to read, and

foremost is his beloved Pug Trump. Now Trump does not seem to have any resemblance to our present-day Pug at all. He is much too big, long legs, quite a nose and definitely not the cobby body we desire today. In fact Wilhelmine Swainson Goodger describes him in her book as "a mongrel if ever there was one". I don't think I could say quite that. Hogarth must have adored Trump to feature him in his self-portrait and other paintings. Maybe that is what many Pugs looked like in his lifetime. Hogarth certainly looks very proud of him in his painting. However, Pug he was. The cropped ears and hanging tongue, the like of which was seen in the 1700s, and the fact that history tells us it was a Pug, means we do accept Trump as a Pug of that period of time. Hogarth's head study of Trump, which hangs in the Kennel Club in London, is a lovely picture from an artist's point of view but I very much doubt if Trump would win a first prize at a show today. Hogarth and Trump had an extremely close relationship and when Trump died he was buried in the garden of Hogarth's house in Chiswick, London. Trump was not the only Pug that Hogarth owned – in fact he had a predecessor, "a light colour'd Dutch Dog with a black muzzle and answers to the name of Pugg", and he was succeeded in the 1750s by another, named Crab. Such was Hogarth's love of Trump that his likeness with him was caricatured in 1753-4. Attributed to Paul Standby, it is entitled *Puggs Graces*, and shows Hogarth with the hind-legs of a dog seated at his easel. Aiming to be anonymous it is signed 'A.C. Inv. et Sculp.' and beneath the print is the rhyme, "Behold a Wretch who nature form'd in spight,
Scorn'd by the Wise; he gave the Fools

The Painter and his Pug (1746)
By William Hogarth.
Courtesy: Tate Gallery, London.

Delight,
Yet not contented in his Sphere to move
Beyond mere Instinct, and his Senses drove
From false Examples hop'd to pilfer Fame
And scribl'd nonsense in his daubing Name.
Deformity her Self his Figures place,
She spreads an Uglines on every Face
He then admires their Ellegance and Grace
Dunce Connoisseurs extol the Author Pugg,
The sensles, tasteless, impudent, Hum Bugg."
     Hogarth himself was often described as a

satirist and this is particularly shown in the way he altered his own self-portrait in his engraving *The Bruiser* (1763). The poet Churchill had criticised the self-portrait, comparing the likeness between Hogarth and his Pug, Trump (Since this was not the first occasion that this had happened, perhaps there was something in this resemblance.) To retaliate, Hogarth crudely replaced himself with a drunken bear representing Churchill, his enemy at that time, but Trump remained in the foreground, with a slight smirk on his face, urinating over one of Churchill's pamphlets. Hogarth was so fond of the Pug dog that he introduced him into many of his paintings even before he painted his self-portrait. *The Wollaston Family* (1730) has a perky little Pug in the foreground. *The Fountaine Family* (1731) has a little fat puppy, again in the foreground. *The Strode Family* features Trump (no doubt). *Captain Lord Graham in his Cabin* (1742) shows a Pug sitting up on his hind legs wearing his master's wig, standing to attention with a scroll of paper for a musket in his paws, as he pretends to sing a song from a sheet of music propped up against a silver beaker. Whether this was the Captain's Pug or Hogarth's is not known, but certainly he has a prominent part in the picture. Then there is *A Rake's Progress* (1732-1734), a story told in a series of eight oil on canvas paintings. In the fifth picture Rake marries a rich old maid for her money. The painting shows the groom with his bride, withered and ugly and she with only one eye. Hogarth introduced two Pugs, the dog licking and courting the bitch who, in resemblance to the old maid, also has one eye. Such was Hogarth's sense of humour.

Then of course we have *The House of*

Cards (1730) featuring the little black Pug. One can see that he is full of the character of a Pug but very leggy and fine boned, and body and head conformation is difficult to see. The interesting thing about this picture is the Pug being black. So often we read that black Pugs were unheard of in this country until 1886 when Lady Brassey brought them back with her from one of her Eastern voyages, but in Hogarth's painting we see one 150 years earlier. Queen Victoria is also said to have had a Black Pug in 1850, so it appears still a mystery as to when and how the black Pug first appeared.

GOYA (1746-1828)

I think the most charming Pug from any painting in the past is the one by the Spanish artist Francisco José de Goya in his painting of the Marquesa de Pontejos. This painting is so typical of the Pug of today, even to the raised foot – but here again, as with Hogarth's paintings, it has cropped ears in keeping with that period. Still, it is a very delightful picture which now hangs in America's National Gallery of Art in Washington, DC.

GEORGE KNAPTON

There is a delightful painting which features a Pug that hangs in Hampton Court Palace, London. It is by George Knapton and is part of the Royal Collection. The painting depicts Augusta, Princess of Wales, wearing a black veil to show her recent widowhood, sitting with her nine children. In the background hangs a portrait of her deceased husband Frederick, Prince of Wales, wearing his Robes of State. Seated second from the left is young George, the new Prince of Wales who succeeded his grandfather to become

George III of England. In the front of the painting is the Pug. Charlotte Princess of Mecklenburg-Strelitz, wife of George III, was very fond of the breed and kept quite a number.

PHILIP RICHARD MORRIS
(1838-1902)

Philip Richard Morris painted a most charming picture titled *Quite Ready*. It features a little girl, dressed for a party, sitting at the bottom of a staircase waiting for her carriage. Beside her patiently, yet quite alert, sits her Pug, as though waiting to go with her (I wonder if he did?). It is a lovely picture, one that I am pleased to have a large print of hanging in my home. I expect many more Pug owners also have the pleasure of this delightful painting to look at and admire.

Quite Ready. By Philip Richard Morris (1838-1902).

CHARLES BURTON BARBER
(1845-1894)

Another great artist who included the Pug in many of his paintings was Charles Burton Barber. Born in Great Yarmouth in 1845, he studied at the Academy Schools. In 1866, at the age of 21, he exhibited his first paintings at the Royal Academy. He was a great animal painter and most of his work included animals and children. During his lifetime he painted many of Queen Victoria's favourite dogs and several of these works included Her Majesty's grandchildren. Among his collection is a lovely painting of *A Family of Pugs*, seven in all, owned by Queen Victoria. There is also *Basco, Prince Battenberg's favourite Pug aged 9*, a water-colour, painted in 1886.

A Family of Pugs. By Charles Burton Barber (1877). A painting of Queen Victoria's Pugs which hangs in Osborne House.

Courtesy: The Royal Collection. Her Majesty The Queen

Both these paintings are in the Royal Collection at Osborne House on the Isle of Wight. Others that he painted are *Foul in Hand*, *River Puggy* (1828), *Pug, Yorkshire Terrier and Italian Greyhound* (1879), *Blonde and Brunette* (1879), *Prince Alesa of Battenberg* and *Prince Drino and Princess Eva of Battenberg*. Each of these pictures shows a Pug, and all are most delightful paintings. My favourite of all his paintings is *A Mute Appeal*. The blind man's stick can just be seen in the right hand corner of the painting. The look of sadness and, at the same time, expression of gratitude of his dog, in contrast to the snooty, pompous behaviour of the lovely, aristocratic Pug has been so beautifully portrayed in the painting. That for me is most delightful. Unfortunately I couldn't get a copy suitable for printing in this book.

GOURLAY STEELL (1819-1890)

Gourlay Steell was a member of the Royal Scottish Academy and was Queen Victoria's official animal painter for Scotland following the death of Landseer. In about 1867 he produced the well-known Pug painting titled *The Celebrated Drumpellier Pugs* which was exhibited at the Royal Academy in 1873. This famous painting was sold at Christie's in Scotland in April 1988 for £18,000 ($27,000). It was included again in the sale at Christie's in London in February 1990 and was expected to fetch between £20,000 ($30,000) and £30,000 ($45,000). It remained unsold, and is said to be too well-known by the market for its own good. This is a most delightful picture showing eight Pugs.

A Pug painted on vellum. Austria (c 1880)
This painting was originally on a tambourine. It belongs to the Lawson Johnson Family. It has been handed down through the generations and still hangs in their house.

Pugs painted on glass (1885).

Sea Scene. A mural painted by Sophie Mount on a wall at her home in Huntingdon, Cambridgeshire.

COLLECTABLES

During the Victorian era it was said that no genteel lady would be seen without her Pug Dog. This gave artists every opportunity to make use of the popularity of the breed. They printed Christmas cards, birthday cards, Valentine cards and even cigar bands and Christmas cracker stickers depicting a Pug, all of which are greatly sought after by collectors today.

NEEDLEWORK

In the nineteenth century, when there was no television to watch and the age of 'sports leisure' had not arrived, when wealth meant that large numbers of middle-class ladies could employ servants to look after their homes and their children, needlework became an alternative way of passing their time. It was fashionable for young ladies to become accomplished in the art of sewing, starting first with their

A sketch of the Pug Dog especially drawn for the author, Ellen Brown, by Haro Hodson, the cartoonist who regularly features this cariacature in the Daily Mail.

A selection of modern day tapestries in the style of the Victorian era, owned by Alison Mount and worked by her mother.

samplers. The needlewomen took to embroidery and tapestry and the Pug could be seen on cushions, fire-screens, footstools and pouffes. The Victorian ladies had plenty of charts and patterns to choose from and they gained their inspiration from books of drawings, of which Landseer was one such artist, with his fine study of animals and particularly of Queen Victoria's pets. Unfortunately I have found no drawings of Pugs by Landseer. I have read that in 1894 a Mr E. Jessup exhibited some beautiful point work at the Burlington Gallery which included *Bully the Pug*. Bully was the Pug belonging to Queen Victoria's granddaughter.

Today that interest has returned and Pug owners are now repeating what our ancestors did in Victorian days. Ladies like to relax from the hustle and bustle of everyday life and return to those serene days as they sit and work their tapestries and needlepoints. Needleworkers of today have even greater choice than their Victorian counterparts. There are many 'kits' of Pug tapestries and needlepoint available today, complete with wool, chart and canvas or embroidery silk and pica. It is not difficult to find them on stalls at most dog shows. Once again Victorian-style tapestries of Pugs are appearing in modern

homes, as pictures, cushions, stools and fire-screens, just as they did over one hundred years ago.

CERAMICS

Models of the Pug have been created in porcelain, stone, clay and brass, in fact in anything available for modelling, and the different versions are amazing. Of course the most expensive and sought-after are exclusive Meissen porcelain (often miscalled Dresden porcelain) and these fetch fantastic prices. The Meissen factory in Saxony is one of the oldest in Europe manufacturing porcelain. It was under Augustus the Strong that two chemists set about trying to unfold the secret elements of this fine type of pottery ware which had been known in the East for many centuries. By 1710 they had discovered a formula. In 1731 Johann J. Kändler joined the factory and was responsible for animal models. When Augustus died in 1733 the factory was handed over to Count Heinrich von Brühl, minister at the court of Augustus III of Hanover. Both Kändler and von Brühl were Pug owners, which must account for the many models that were produced. It is said that these models were created from life studies, and one is known to have been the pet Pug of Count Heinrich von Brühl.

ABOVE: *Painted terracotta Pug. Germany (1850-1860).*

LEFT: *Terracotta Pugs. Germany. 1850-1860. (Notice the glass eyes.)*

All Meissen and early models of the Pug show the cropped ears. Thank goodness the desire to crop a Pug's ears ceased in later years – probably due to the intervention of Queen Victoria, but we have no proof of this.

At an auction in London quite recently some most beautiful antique Pugs were for sale. One pair of Meissen Pug models (c1880) in the style of J.J. Kändler depicted the Pugs seated, wearing ribbon collars stitched with bells. The Pug bitch has a puppy creeping out from under her paws. Their coats are enriched in dark brown and tan. There were others, not quite so valuable, probably because of slight damage. An Austrian terracotta model of a Pug (1880), seated, with collar and fitted with glass eyes, was again slightly damaged but fetched top price. Most outstanding of all was an original pair of Meissen Pugs (c 1740). Even though with a slight repair, these were very highly priced. What if these ornaments could tell us their stories – who had owned them over the last 100 to 150 years and where they have been? This collection actually came from Geneva and

the prices ranged from £300 ($450) to £6000 ($9,000) for the Pug models.

It does seem to be that once the Meissen potteries started to produce their Pug models this became a popular theme with other potteries. In England the earliest models were made in the Chelsea and Chelsea-Derby factories. Royal Worcester, Rockingham, Staffordshire and Bow factories, among others, were soon in the market for Pug models. What were being sold in the early 1900s for a few shillings are now fetching top prices. Collecting Pug models can be quite expensive but the interest is there today and any Pug owner is "over the moon" to suddenly come across a rare piece that no-one else has. Every last penny is scraped together to possess it. Such is the enthusiasm.

One very interesting prize possession at the Victoria and Albert Museum is a model of a Pug which is believed to be a Chelsea Pug that is a close copy, perhaps even a cast, of the terracotta model of William Hogarth's favourite dog, Trump, by Roubiliac. It measures 12.4cm high and 26.7cm long. The original terracotta model

TOP: Meissen Bitch with Puppy and Dog figures wearing blue collars and gilt bells. Impressed Mark, 19th Century.

LEFT: Meissen Apricot Bitches.

and Roubiliac's bust of Hogarth were in Hogarth's house, where they remained until the death of the painter's widow. Hogarth's bust was purchased by John Hunter from the sale of effects of Hogarth's wife and in turn he sold it to Samuel Ireland, author of *Graphic Illustrations of Hogarth* (1799). In his book, Samuel Ireland states: "I have introduced, beneath the bust, the figure of Hogarth's dog Trump, modelled by the same artist. It had been jocularly observed by him, that there was a close resemblance betwixt his own countenance and that of his favourite dog, who was his faithful friend and companion for many years and for whom he had conceived a greater share of attachment than is usually bestowed on these domestic animals. I make no apology for the introduction of his portrait to the notice of the reader, because the attentions, of which the master thought him worthy, have in a manner (if I may be allowed to say so much concerning a dog) conferred a sort of dignity upon his memory."

Records lose track of the terracotta bust of Hogarth and that of Trump after 1832 but it is understood that Roubiliac sold plaster casts of the Pug. The plaster cast passed to Wedgwood and, although none exist now, there are records in the Wedgwood archives of 'A Pug Dog'. Later in Wedgwood's Auctions of 1781 there appears 'two Pug dogs, from Hogarth' and 'a pair of Pug dogs from a favourite dog of Hogarth's'. Wedgwood employed modellers competent in reversing models so they could produce a pair.

To return to the Pug model at the Victoria and Albert Museum. Research has been done to try to date this model and J.V.G. Mallet reported in a V & A Museum Bulletin in 1967 that it is an English porcelain figure as intriguing as any in their collection. Though unmarked, this piece seems datable to the late triangle or early raised anchor period, about 1747-50, on grounds of paste and glue. By 1751-3 Chelsea was producing raised anchor marked figures of Pugs after Meissen originals.

In the mid-1960s there were also two enamelled figures of Pugs, one larger than the other, in Mr T.G. Burn's collection at Rous Lench. They had no factory marks but were also proved to have derived from Roubiliac's terracotta. The larger model, about 13cm high and 27.7cm long, is ascribed, on the evidence of the paste and glaze, to the earliest years of Chelsea (about 1745-7). The smaller model, about 5.7cm high and 7.8cm long, has been attributed to Chelsea around 1745-7. Both these Pugs face the same way and it is thought that maybe each was part of a pair. Incidentally the Museum's Pug is facing the other way. The findings have revealed that the Pug figures at Rous Lench are two of the earliest enamelled porcelain figures ever made in England.

New models are often seen around but it

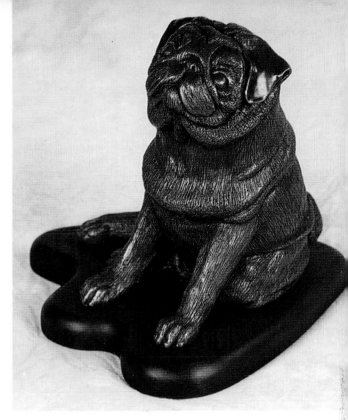

The Seated Pug. A half-size bronze Pug by Don Wiedon (modern). Winner of the Best Pug entry in the 1992 Art Show At The Dog Show, Wieheta, Kansas.

is the old ones that the demand is for, and the older the better. One can feel the history around them and one's imagination takes one into the past to wonder who and how many people have owned what is now your precious Pug model. They are real treasures.

9 BACKGROUND TO THE MODERN PUG

At the turn of the 16th century the Pug was much in demand. However, during the hundred years between the reign of William the Silent in Holland and the arrival in England of William and Mary of Orange, there was a decline. Then the aristocracy in England followed their new King and Queen's love of the Pug and, from 1688, this breed became popular once again. By the early 1700s Pugs had found their way all over Europe.

THE FIRST REGISTRATIONS

The first dog show to include a class specifically for Pugs was at Birmingham in December 1860, but there were no entries. At Leeds, in July 1861, a Mr Brown (no relation to the author as far as I know!) won with Bloom and Mr H. Gilbert was second (no name of the dog is recorded). The earliest breeder of distinction must be Mr Mayhew, owner of Click, one of the most talked of Pugs in the history of the breed. In *The Dog Book* (1906), Mr James Watson wrote: "Click's parents – Lamb and Moss – were Chinese beyond dispute. They were captured in the Emperor of China's Palace during the siege of Pekin in 1867 or

1868, and were brought to England by the then Marquis of Wellesley, I think. Anyhow, they were given to a Mrs St. John, who brought them several times to our house. Alike as two peas, they were solid apricot fawn without a suspicion of white: had lovely heads and expressions; but unlike their son, they were close to the ground, and a shade long in body." This story had been related to Mr Watson by Mr Mayhew's son. Lamb and Moss, therefore, were the parents of Click, although the date of his birth has been difficult to ascertain but is believed to be about 1867. Click was an apricot fawn and was an outstanding sire of the early days. It is said that if we were able to trace pedigrees back over 100 years or more, we would eventually find Click somewhere there in the pedigrees of all Pugs of today.

THE REPETITION OF NAMES

Breeding lines, and the dogs one reads about in research, become quite a problem because names such as Click, Lamb, Moss, Punch, Rose and Judy appear over and over again, where breeders repeated names in later litters. Researching at the Kennel Club quite recently I meticulously noted the names of the Pugs listed from 1859 to 1873 and found twelve Topsys, ten Princes, nine Punches, five Blondins, five Victors and four Judys, as well as numerous names with two entries. This went on into the first volume of the *Kennel Club Stud Book* in 1874, where Pugs registered were: four Princes, six Punches, two Pippins, three Judys, three Tobys and five Topsys; some with pedigrees, some without. One does not know whether they were different dogs or the same ones with repeated entries. It certainly made a difference when it was decided to use prefixes. This can be substantiated by the article written in the *Kennel Gazette* issued by the Kennel Club in October 1885: "Until within very late years it would have been quite impossible to form anything like a pedigree table of the Pug family; and this was not because there was any want of antiquity in the breed, or because it was of recent manufacture, as all of its associations point to exactly the opposite direction. It is possibly the most aristocratic breed in the whole 'Stud Book'. The belongings of lords and ladies, and always cared for with so much jealous guarding as to preclude the chances of being crossed with plebeian strains. It has so existed for a period to be counted almost by centuries, but no one kept any record of pedigrees, and when the shows became prominent institutions, it was the fashion to talk of Mr Morrison's strain, said to have been procured from the royal household, and the Willoughby D'Eresby breed, but the public had simply the names of a few from the above sources, together with the others without any stated pedigree."

The first recorded names of Champions that I have in my records were in 1886 when there were five Champions. These were Mrs M.A. Foster's Ch. Diamond, Mrs L. Booth's Ch. Boffin, Mr T. Wilkinson's Ch. Second Challenger, Mr W.L. Sheffield's Ch. Stingo Sniffles and Mrs R.H. Dennes' Ch. Little Gipsy Queen. To become a Champion a dog must have won seven first prizes at shows registered in or for *The Kennel Club Stud Book*. Three of the seven first prizes had to be won in the Challenge classes and one, at least, of the Challenge prizes had to be won at the Kennel Club's own shows or those of the National Dog Show, Birmingham. There were no Challenge Certificates, as we know them today, awarded until 1896.

The Kennel Club was formed in 1873 and the Pug Dog Club ten years later in 1883 with Miss M.A.E. Holdsworth from Leeds as the first secretary. The Pug Dog Club was one of the first to be registered with the Kennel Club. A Breed Standard was adopted when the PDC was formed. This had several similarities to the Standard produced by the canine writer and judge Hugh Dalziel and has changed very little since. So with a club, club members, breeders and a Breed Standard, we hear more about Champions. This was the real beginning of shows and exhibitors.

THE FIRST PUG DOG CLUB SHOWS
The Pug Dog Club held its first show at the Royal Aquarium, Westminster, on Tuesday, Wednesday and Thursday, June 16, 17, 18, 1885. The judge was Mr James Berrie who, incidentally, was also the president of the Club. The entrance fee for each dog was 10 shillings and there were 151 entries from 94 Pugs. In the catalogue many of the Pugs were advertised for sale, with prices ranging from £12 ($19) right up to two that were for sale for £1000 ($1650). Although many of the handlers

were men, it was observed that at this show it was obvious that the Pug was a favourite with the ladies, as their presence was very prominent. It was quite usual at a show like this to find that the Pugs were adorned in jewellery. It was particularly noted that Mrs Rennie's Lion, who was in Class 3, was wearing a garland of turquoise beads. How annoying for the poor little Pug!

Following the shows of 1885 it was written in the Press that the size of the Pugs was obviously prominent in the minds of the breeders, but it was felt that the establishment of the PDC was helping to keep them small. Certainly the Club must have been having some influence on the quality of the Pug because the *Kennel Gazette* article of 1885 concluded by saying: "There are other recent winners by dogs with no public records, and with only what might be called private pedigrees, but that they are perfectly bred is shown by their produce. Pug breeders have beautiful grounds to exercise their skill upon, and there is no more interesting and satisfactory breed to take up than these blue-blooded little companions of fashion." So the Club flourished. At the Pug Dog Club's second annual show in 1886 there were 76 Pugs with 141 entries. The third annual show followed in 1887 and there were 70 Pugs with 134 entries.

Records of the time were certainly most confusing. I wonder if the Mr Brown who won at Birmingham in 1860 could be the same Mr W.E. Brown who, on August 4th, 1885, bred Stately from Beau out of Bonnie Princess. Mr W.L. Sheffield owned a Stately, so did Mrs Lyons, whose Stately was awarded his Championship title in 1889. I don't know if this was the same dog with a change of owner or a different dog. Mr W.L. Sheffield was also the owner

of Ch. Stingo Sniffles, an early Champion who was said to be a very perfect Pug of the day. According to an advertisement, Stingo Sniffles was a silver fawn with extraordinary wrinkles, jet black toe-nails and weighing about 13 lbs. In one source I have recorded that Ch. Little Count became a Champion in 1887 and from another I discovered that his litter sister, owned by Mrs C. S. Brittain, gained her title in 1888. Miss M.A.E. Holdsworth, who was the Pug Dog Club's first secretary, had the honour of being the first lady to judge at a dog show. She judged at the Maidstone Show in 1886 where it is said: "It was rather novel to see a judge in a sealskin jacket with a spray of flowers and a bonnet." She also judged Pugs at the Scarborough Show in 1887.

END OF THE 19TH CENTURY
The main breeders at the end of the nineteenth century were Mrs C. Houlker, Mr H. Maule, Mrs T. Proctor and Miss L.E. Harris. These breeders were still showing their Pugs when the Kennel Club first started to issue Challenge Certificates in 1896. Ch. Dowager, owned by Miss Holdsworth, appears in many pedigrees of the time. He was the sire of Ch. Queen Rose, owned by Miss Houlker, and of Ch. Diamond, born on May 14th 1882, who was bred and owned by Mrs M.A. Foster. Ch. Diamond was winning shows in 1886. From a mating of Ch. Queen Rose and Ch. Diamond, Mrs Houlker bred her first Pug, Ch. Loris, in 1884. As you can see from his interesting pedigree, Ch. Loris gained his title in 1888. Ch. Royal Duke, a son of Ch. Dowager, born August 14th 1886, was bred and owned by Mr H. Maule and was said to have been an ideal Pug of his time. Mr Maule seems to be one of the first

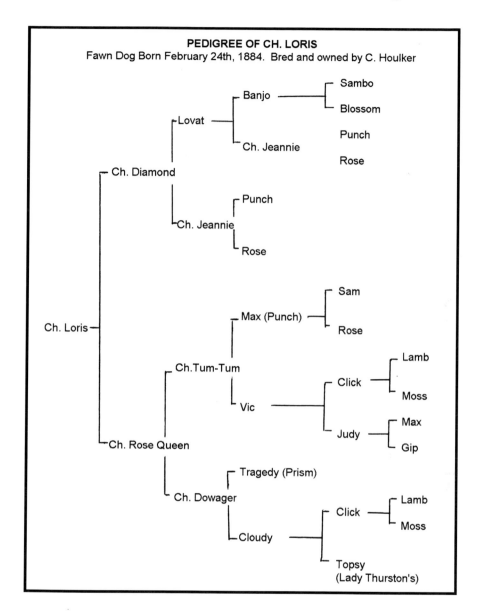

PEDIGREE OF CH. LORIS
Fawn Dog Born February 24th, 1884. Bred and owned by C. Houlker

breeders to use a prefix, Royal, which made identifying breeders easier. Records show that the prefix of Miss L.E. Harris was Finsbury. Ch. Finsbury Major gained his title in 1897. The prefix used by Miss C. Houlker was Haughty. Haughty Madge was exported to America and was one of the first Pugs to be registered there.

Ch. Major of Leeds, owned by Mr T.T. Craven, became one of the UK's earliest Champions, in 1893. He won prizes at Crufts in that year and again in 1894. From pictures I have seen he appears to be a lovely specimen of the breed, taking into consideration it was 100 years ago. Although Championship shows began in

1893, Crufts did not become one until 1897. Pugs were first awarded CCs at Crufts a year later. The BOB at Crufts, 1896, was York, owned by Mrs P. Greliche. He was thought to be a thoroughly good dog but, although he was awarded one CC in 1896 and another in 1898, I can find no records of him becoming a Champion. Mention here must be made of Lady Brassey and her great influence on the introduction of the black Pug. More details of this are written in Chapter One on the history of the Pug.

The PDC Show in May, 1890 was held at the Central Hall, Holborn, and the judge was a Mr E. Wallis. This was possibly the first Club Show which had a separate class for blacks. There was another new class at this show, namely one for Best Brace of Pugs. A report on this show said that the classes were well filled except for the puppy class. The quality of the Pugs was consistently good, especially in the Open Bitch Class under 15 lbs. Apparently remarks were made by well-known judges concerning the fact that the nose should be as short as possible, the muzzle should be blunt, square and deep and the lips should not overhang. There was concern that the lippiness was being passed for squareness of muzzle, and froggy expressions were being produced by a narrow receding underjaw which was most undesirable. Apparently there was a delay in judging Pugs at this show because the KC scales were out of order. So it appears that Pugs used to be weighed at shows. I wonder when and why this stopped and what the reaction would be if it were reintroduced.

EARLY 20TH CENTURY

At the turn of the century the names of more breeders appear and among the top

Miss Rosa Little: A dedicated lady of Pugs for over forty years. Secretary of the PDC for 16 years. Resigned in 1925 and became President. Photograph 1911.

ones were Mrs H. Andrews (Swarland), Mrs J. Neish (Laws), Mrs M. Benson, Miss Rosa Little (Baronshalt), Mrs Hampden-Shaw (Turret) and Mrs Warden-Gowling. From 1901 to 1916 Mrs M. Benson owned nine Champions. She campaigned Ch. Prince Puggawug to his title in 1908. He was a winner at Crufts in 1909 and again in 1910. Puggawug was the first puppy bred by Miss May Woolridge and was an outstanding stud dog. It is said that nearly every bitch at that time visited him. He became the sire of numerous excellent winning and Champion Pugs. Mrs Benson also campaigned Ch. Dollaleen who gained 21 CCs from 1909 to 1915.

Miss May Woolridge was a renowned breeder and judge of Pugs at the beginning of this century. From her own Ch. Lord

Delamy, a black dog, she bred Ch. Prince Pipkin, an excellent black dog who won 19 CCs by the time he was four years old. Another Champion bred and owned by Miss Woolridge was Ch. Crook of Gold, a fawn dog. Baronshalt was the prefix of Miss Rosa Little, a lady dedicated to the Pugs who shared her life for over forty years. The first Champion that she bred was Ch. Sigelinda of Baronshalt, descended from Ch. Confidence. Another very successful Pug that she owned was Ch. Betty of Pomfret, descended from her own Baronshalt line. She was Best Bitch at Crufts in 1904, 1905 and 1906. Ch. Lady Mimosa was a most beautiful black bitch. The last Champion that she showed was Ch. Caroli of Baronshalt, a black dog noted for his good head. From my records she made up seven Champions and was awarded CCs with many more. Her kennels had a great influence on the breed throughout the 1920s and 1930s. She became secretary of the Pug Dog Club, a position that she held for sixteen years until 1925 when she resigned and became president. In 1926 she held a garden party at her home in Twickenham for the PDC with treasure hunts and competitions for the Pugs and their owners. Mrs Hampden-Shaw bred nine Champions in her kennels under the prefix Turret. These were mostly from her own sires. The Turret prefix was famous wherever Pugs were known and the quality of them was said to be quite outstanding.

Mrs Recketts, with the prefix Boscobel, was another top breeder at this time. She bred five Champions during the years 1910 to 1914. Her kennels were purchased in 1915 by Miss H. C. Couper. Ch. Rocket of Boscobel, Ch. Rapture of Boscobel and Ch. Kittie Sparkes continued to win CCs with

their new owner. Miss Couper, a breeder of Pugs for many years, always took great consideration in her breeding and produced many fine Pugs. Notable ones from the 1920s were Ch. Narcissus of Otter, winning 7 CCs, and Ch. Dancing Dickerine of Otter. Miss Couper married and became Mrs L. Lake.

At the outbreak of the First World War in 1914, such names as Houlker, Benson, Little, Hampton-Shaw, Reckett, Demaine, and Couper were attending shows and making up Champions. Registrations in 1916 were 49 fawn and 46 black Pugs. The numbers were declining because of the war and by 1918 only seventeen fawns and nine blacks were registered. By 1919, once the war was over, 23 fawn and 38 black Pugs were registered – now they were on the increase. Challenge Certificates ceased to be awarded during the Great War years, but were resumed in 1920, by which time new breeders were entering shows.

One such breeder, owner and handler of the 1920s was Mrs Prowett-Ferdinands. Her first Champion was the black dog Ch. Young Scotland, who gained his title in 1920. As the sire of Ch. Dark Ducas he had a great influence on the Pugs of the day and of the future. Mrs Prowett-Ferdinands continued to have excellent stock, breeding seven Champions of great renown between 1920 and 1934. Another breeder who influenced the development of the Pug during this time was Miss Blanche Thomson with her Fairlea kennels which included Ch. Fairlea Antonia. There was also Mrs Vincent Curtis, the breeder of Ch. Miss Penelope, who was an outstanding black bitch by Massa Sambo of Broadway out of Ch. Penelope. Ch. Miss Penelope continued to produce first-class stock and must be considered the backbone of many excellent Pugs that followed. Lord Wrottesley, who had no prefix, also had good stock. There really were so many devoted breeders and excellent Pugs during this time – but they are too numerous to mention.

During the years between the two World Wars there were new breeders interested in the Pug. Mrs C. Demaine with her family of blacks, having bred her first Champion, Ch. Dark Diana, in 1909, continued with her successes until 1947. She was awarded fifty-five CCs with fifteen Pugs, making up nine Champions. Ch. Dark Diana, a beautiful black bitch bred by Mrs Demaine, was the foundation of the 'Dark' line of breeding. Ch. Dark Ducas, a fawn dog, gained his title in 1920. His son Ch. Dark Dickory was an outstanding show and stud dog of his time. When he, in turn, was mated to Ch. Miss Penelope, the outcome was Ch. Dark Dragoon and Ch. Master of Inver. Ch. Miss Penelope and her son, Ch. Master of Inver, were owned by Misses Hatrick, Campbell and Morrison. From 1924 to 1938 these three ladies with their Inver prefix received twenty-two CCs with seven Pugs, of which four became Champions.

From the twenties onwards Mrs E.N. Power was winning with her Broadway Pugs. From 1920 to 1933 she was awarded forty-four CCs with seventeen Pugs, making up eight Champions. Perhaps her most famous was her fawn dog, Ch. Lord Tom Noddy of Broadway, who won 9 CCs between 1920 and 1922. Broadway Pugs were known all over the world. At one time Mrs Power had the largest kennel of Pugs in the British Isles and probably in the whole world. Her canine family ran into three figures.

PHIDGITY AND PHILWIL

Miss Susan Graham-Weall started breeding in 1925 and through all her years she must have been the most respected and devoted owner/breeder of the Pug dog and member of the PDC. She was the PDC chairman for many years. Susan was always pleasant and willing to help newcomers and fellow breeders. She travelled overseas many times to many countries where she judged. Her Phidgity Pugs were known world-wide. In 1965 her book on the Pug was first published but is now out of print. She judged Pugs four times at Crufts. The last occasion was in 1986, just three months before she died.

After the end of the Second World War Susan was having fears about losing her line of breeding. Most of her bitches had grown too old to breed from and her stock was getting low. It was then that Mr and Mrs W. Williams of Philwil breeding offered Susan a puppy by Mrs Swainston-Goodger's Ch. Silvio of Swainston whose pedigree contained Phidgity breeding. This puppy proved to be a great success and became Ch. Phidgity Phyllis. Phyllis was mated twice to Ch. Philwil Abbot. The first litter produced Ch. Ducray Phidgity Phyllida and Ch. Phidgity Phyl's Son. In turn, Phyl's Son produced Ch. Muchmor Jiniwin Jason, bred and owned by Mrs Purcell. Jason had two Champion sons, Ch. Muchmor Cutmil Francis and Ch. Justatwerp of Cedarwood. Twerp was bred by Mrs E. Crane and owned and campaigned by Mrs P. Thorp. Ch. Phidgity Phenella and Ch. Phidgity Philbert were the result of the second mating. So the Phidgities were back amongst the top winning Pugs and continued to be so from then on. They have since been the background of many breeders' stock.

An informal photograph of Miss Susan Graham-Weall with a family of Phidgity Pugs. Susan bred and owned Pugs for over 61 years.

Mr and Mrs W. Williams started their breeding in 1938. They managed to keep their interest in breeding all through the Second World War and worked on the best lines. Success was theirs when in 1945 they bred Ch. Philwil Abbot, one of the best post-war Pugs. He was truly a Pug of top quality, with good bone, large head and apricot fawn coat. He was awarded eight CCs and he proved himself as a good stud dog. His name can still be seen on the pedigrees of Pugs today. Ch. Philwil Amber, his litter sister, was beautiful in all aspects and as feminine as her brother was masculine. Between 1947 and 1962 Mr and Mrs Williams bred fifteen Champions, eight of which were exported. The Phidgities and the Philwils certainly had that desired link to produce the qualities of a good line of breeding. Mrs Wyn Lewis of the Ducray prefix made up five Champions with Phidgity and Philwil breeding. These were Ch. Ducray Phidgity Phyllida, Ch. Phidgity Phenella, Ch. Philwil Josephine, Ch. Ducray Amanda and Ch. Ducray Daniel. The last three were homebred.

In the early 1930s Mrs Wilhelmine Swainston-Goodger's name appears amongst the top breeders. When she mated her first bitch, Giovanna of Swainston, to her black dog, Ch. Prempeh of Hopeworth, the result was a litter of seven puppies including Ch. Thunder Cloud of Swainston. Thunder Cloud was a fawn dog who was BOB at Crufts in 1938. His resounding success in the show ring was to be cut short by the war. Ch. Silvio of Swainston won seven CCs between 1947 and 1949. As I have already mentioned, Silvio was the sire of Susan Graham-Weall's Phidgity Phyllis, the puppy that she got from Mrs Williams. Mrs Swainston-Goodger will always be remembered for the two delightful and interesting books which she wrote on the Pug. It was due to Susan Graham-Weall, Wilhelmine Swainston-Goodger, Mr and Mrs Williams, Miss Atherton and Violet Graham that the breed kept going throughout World War II. Their dedication to the Pug Dog was most loyal, to be able to breed satisfactorily through such trying times.

Mrs Wendy Allen, with her Goldengleam Pugs, left a great influence on the breed. Her Pugs were at the start of the Banchory and the Ryden Pugs. Goldengleam was used with the Edenderry kennels and I see that Elmsleigh and Cedarwood also appear to have Goldengleam somewhere in their pedigrees. Goldengleam Trooper was owned and loved by the Duke and Duchess of Windsor. He was bought by the Duke and Duchess, it is said, after being awarded Best of Breed at Crufts in 1953, but I can find no records of this win. From my

Ch. Silvio of Swainston: Sire of Ch. Phidgity Phyllis. Owned by Wilhelmine Swainston-Goodger.

Ch. Phidgity Phyllis: Dam of Ch. Phidgity Phyl's Son. Bred by Mr and Mrs W. Williams. Owned by Susan Graham-Weall.

Ch. Philwil Abbot: One of the best post-war Pugs; sire of Ch. Phidgity Phyl's Son. Owner/breeder Mr and Mrs W. Williams.

Ch. Phidgity Phyl's Son (Ch. Philwil Abbot – Ch. Phidgity Phyllis). Owned by Susan Graham-Weall.

personal research at the KC, I discovered that it was Goldengleam Shot Silk who was BOB at Crufts, and this was in 1954.

BLACK PUGS

Another dedicated breeder at that time was Mrs Bancroft-Wilson. For many years she was the editor of The Pug Dog Club *Bulletin* and this she did most successfully.

These *Bulletins* are still most interesting and a joy to read. Mrs Bancroft-Wilson's Ch. Blackberry of Longlands was the first of the Longlands successful line of black breeding. In the early 1950s Ladslove of Longlands was at stud and he was the sire of three Champions, Ch. Edenderry Barney Campbell, Ch. Banchory Guinea and Ch. Banchory Sovereign.

Lady Countess Howe bred all black Pugs. She made up her first Champion in 1954 with Ch. Banchory Bluedoor Taffeta. Her next was homebred Ch. Banchory Silk sired by Mrs W. S. Young's homebred Ch. Archibald of Rydens. A repeat mating produced the famous Ch. Banchory Lace. Lace won 27 CCs and was the first and only Pug at that time to win Best in Show at an all-breed Championship show. This was at the Birmingham City show in 1957. In the same year Lace was BOB and Reserve in the Toy Group at Crufts. She was BOB again at Crufts in 1960. Unfortunately neither Silk nor Lace left any progeny. Silk died at a young age while whelping and Lace was never bred from.

I am sure that Mrs W.S. Young will always be remembered for her beautiful black dog, the famous Ch. Archibald of Rydens, born in 1951. He sired seven Champions and many lovely black Pugs. He was a great asset to the breed, as were other stud dogs from the Rydens kennels, namely Ch. Buster of Rydens, Ch. What Oh of Rydens and Ch. Sabu of Rydens. Nine English Champions carried the Rydens prefix as did many others overseas. The Rydens line of breeding was carried through with Miss Mary Larter's Pugs which successfully produced Ch. Rydens Oh My of Babraham, Ch. Rydens Eddie of Babraham, Ch. Bo Bo of Babraham, Ch. Elsa of Babraham and Ch. Solo Tu of Babraham. Mary Larter's first Champion was Ch. Kate of Rydens, litter sister to Mrs Young's Ch. Mandy of Rydens.

Mrs Violet Graham of the Edenderry prefix owned her first Pug when she was nine years of age and he lived until he was fifteen years old. In 1919 she had another but it was not until 1923 that she started to breed. In those days she lived and showed

Ch. Banchory Lace: Winner of the Toy Group, Windsor Championship Show, 1956 – one of the best black Pugs ever to be shown. Owned by Lorna Countess Howe.

Pugs in Ireland; she eventually moved to England in 1952. She continued breeding and showing both black and fawns, making up seven English Champions. Amongst them was Ch. Edenderry Barney Campbell (Crufts BOB in 1958), sired by Ladslove of Longlands as I have previously mentioned. Ch. Edenderry Shauna (fawn) was Crufts BOB winner and Reserve in the Toy Group in 1963. Ch. Edenderry the O'Donovan (fawn) was BOB at Crufts in 1965. Pugs from her kennels were also Champions in America, Finland, Sweden and Norway. When I first knew Mrs Graham, in the mid 1960s, she was a dear old lady. She had never had any children of her own but, strange as it may seem, we all knew her as Granny Graham. I don't know why, perhaps it was because she was the Granny of the breed at that time. Miss Nancy Sloan was just fifteen years of age when she first started to work for Mrs Graham in Ireland. She started as a parlour maid and stayed

*Mrs Violet Graham,
photographed in her
early years. Mrs
Graham was a breeder
of Pugs for over 50
years, first in Ireland,
then after World War
II in England.*

*Mrs V. Graham judging at the LKA Championship Show, 1955, with Mrs H. Green and
Raydium Little Susie of Harloo (left) and Mrs A. Cotes with Ch. Cobury Sammy of
Goldengleam.*

Ch. Edenderry Shauna: BoB and Res. Best Toy Group, Crufts, 1963. Breeder/Owner Miss V. Graham.

Pauline Thorp with Ch. Cedarwood Blunshills Nimrod: BoB and Winner of Toy Group, Crufts, 1967. Seen here receiving the award from HRH Duchess of Gloucester.

with her all her life, becoming her companion and kennel maid. She showed many of the Edenderry Pugs as well as breeding some of her own with equal success. Ch. Edenderry Tara's Harp was bred by Nancy Sloan and owned by Miss Nehring. Ch. Edenderry Padriac, also bred by Nancy, was owned by Tom Gessey, as was Ch. Edenderry Dunboyne. These were all fawns.

THE PEAK OF PUG BREEDING
Miss G. Atherton, of the Cedarwood prefix, bred and showed many successful Pugs in the early 1930s. Pauline Thorp joined her in 1934 as help and stayed with her until she died in 1957. Pauline then took over the Pugs and the prefix. She made up seven Champions. One was Ch. Justatwerp of Cedarwood bred by Mrs Crane. He was most successful in the show ring and was a good sire. I myself mated my foundation bitch to Twerp and she presented me with six lovely bitches and

one handsome dog. Pauline's highlight was in 1967 when Ch. Cedarwood Blunshill Nimrod was the first Pug to win the Toy Group at Crufts. He was a dog with a very determined personality. Ch. Cedarwood Willopop Isa Wonderboy was just the opposite. I don't think he particularly liked shows, for he never looked very happy, but he proved to be a great stud dog. He sired seven Champions and was grandsire to thirteen Champions. Pauline was a very knowledgeable person in the Pug breed. She was the one most people would turn to for advice and was very helpful to newcomers. She was the breed

Ch. Dingleberry Vega: Top Pug Dog 1974, 1975 and 1976. Bred by Mrs Marsden and Mr and Mrs Pickard. Owned by Linda Appleton.   Photo: Diane Pearce

Ch. Taceham Bee's Knees: Daughter of Ch. Dingleberry Vega. Breeder/owner Robin Chandler.

Photo: Diane Pearce.

correspondent for *Our Dogs* for many years. Pauline and her husband Ted forever had an open door at Alton in Hampshire for any Pug owner who was passing by.

Wonderboy was the sire of Ch. Dingleberry Vega. Vega was bred by Mrs Marsden and Mr and Mrs Pickard and owned and campaigned by Miss L. Appleton. He was top Pug dog for three consecutive years 1974, 1975 and 1976. He won fifteen CCs, was Reserve Best in Show at two Championship shows and won the Toy Group at five Championship shows, including Crufts in 1977. Mrs M.

Cummings, another successful show person, owned five Champions, the most successful being Ch. Hazelbridge Paul, bred by Mrs M. Pitt. Paul was awarded twelve CCs, Best Pug at the PDC Championship show for three years running and BOB at Crufts in 1961. He produced three English Champions, eight American Champions, one Canadian Champion and one South African Champion. Mrs Cummings also owned Ch. Heighington Bandleader and Ch. Cerne Spendthrift of Doms, both Paul's sons, and Ch. Sheafdon Ranger of Doms, a black

Bath Champiohship Show, 1962. Judge: Pauline Thorp. Monica Cummings with Cerne Spendthrift of Doms (left), Best Opp Sex, and Mrs H. Haywood with Spreadcombe Cutmil Auriga, BoB.

dog. Not any of them were homebred. Mrs Coleman made up her first Champion in 1958, Ch. Cerne Taurus, sired by Ch. Hazelbridge Paul. He in turn sired five Champions. Other Champions bred by Mrs Coleman were Ch. Cerne Spendthrift of Doms, Ch. Cerne Flamenco, Ch. Cerne Chalumeau, Ch. Cerne Cymbal and Ch. Cerne Bright Star. Bright Star was owned and campaigned by Mrs M. Housey after Mrs Coleman's death in 1974.

Ch. Cerne Taurus: Sire of five English Champions. Breeder/owner Mrs C. Coleman.

Then there was Mrs F. Cooke, known as Cookie, with her Greentubs prefix. She bred both blacks and fawns, making up Champions in both colours and sent some overseas. Ch. Jet Black of Greentubs, sired by Ch. Banchory Sovereign, was BOB at Crufts in 1964. When she was mated to Joe Braddon's Ch. Tertius Inkpen of Pyebeta she produced Ch. Black Nugget of Greentubs. Ch. Greentubs Mulligan, bred by Mr H.E. Ramsden, sired Jean Manifold's first Champion Hyrcania Afra. Mrs Washington-Hibbert also bred both fawns and blacks. She had three Champions, Ch. Normpug Petal, Ch. Normpug China Rose and Ch. Normpug Black Beauty. Mrs Nancy Gifford's lovely stud dogs Ch. Stormie of Martlesham, Ch. Tempest of Martlesham, and Ch. Yardi of Martlesham had a lot to offer the breed, as did Ch. Bronnie of Martlesham, sire of Ch. Maroden Megelwin, bred by Marjorie Odenbriet. Stormie sired seven Champions, one being Ch. Cedarwood Blunshill Nimrod. Ch. Yardi of Martlesham was Stormie's son and he in turn produced Ch. Paglesham Sage. Michael Quinney's Ch. Adoram Cinderfella of Pallas, who was BIS at LKA in 1969, was also by Stormie. When Elizabeth Elbourn mated Olive Beauty of Bournle to Stormie she got two Champions in one litter, Ch. Genevieve of Bournle and Ch. Ivanhoe of Bournle. Ivanhoe was owned and campaigned by Mr

Pictured (left to right): Ch. Bronnie of Martlesham, Ch. Tempest of Martlesham, Ch. Stormie of Martlesham and Ch. Yardi of Martlesham.

Summing up the past: Blond and Brunette (1879) by Charles Burton Barber (1845-1894).

The present-day Pug.
        Photo courtesy: Solihull Times.

and Mrs Judson. Mrs L. Green with the prefix Harloo bred many successful Pugs both black and fawn. Quite a number were exported. She showed Ch. Mirandus Invader of Harloo to gain his title before he was exported to America. He was bred by Mrs J. Greenwood. Mrs Green was a very helpful member of the PDC particularly during her time as the cup steward. Joan Greenwood was another very active member of the PDC. She was chairman for a number of years and gave loyal service as a member of the committee. It was at her home 'Three Ponds' that the garden parties were first started in 1969 and they were held there annually until she moved. These parties are still held every year at different members' homes. Joan's prefix Mirandus was on many a good Pug's pedigree both in blacks and fawns.

Mrs Purcell succeeded in making up four Muchmor Champions, Ch. Muchmor Jiniwin Jason, Ch. Muchmor Cutmil Francis, Ch. Edenderry Bluebell and Ch. Muchmor Buff Orpington of Pyebeta. All were used successfully at stud. Major and Mrs R. Gibson had a great influence on the

breed with their Elmsleigh Pugs. Their last one was Ch. Eastonite Arthur of Elmsleigh who was later sold and went to live in Sweden. Major Gibson was the PDC secretary for a number of years in the 1960s.

Mr and Mrs Laver were very much involved in the NPDC. Mr Laver was their secretary for some years. Mrs Laver had some lovely Pugs including Ch. Alava Victory Roll. Ch. Alava Pirouette, the last Champion that she bred, was sold as a puppy to Mr and Mrs I. Brown (no relation to the author) who were new to Pugs at that time and who had the good fortune to make up their first Pug. Miss J. Haggie was well known for her beautiful blacks, Ch. Sheafdon Midnight Frolic, Ch. Sheafdon Midnight Feast and Ch. Sheafdon Pal Joey of Pizarro, as well as successful ones sent overseas. Miss A. Gretton was a very successful Pug breeder for many years but kept her own kennels small. She exported to many countries where the Hazelbridge prefix can be found on the pedigrees of many Pugs of early breeders.

10 *PUGS TODAY*

We now approach what must be the pinnacle for the Pug Dog. In 1962 the Kennel Club registered 1,668 Pugs. This was the largest registration figure ever. Classes for shows were well filled and it really was something to make up a Champion. In those days one was breeding and showing for many years before one's chances came to own a Champion. So from here I will try to give some idea of the breeders and lovely Pugs that have taken us through to the present day.

ADORAM, DILLYPIN AND PARAMIN

I well remember Michael Quinney in the big ring at Crufts 1966 when, having won BOB with his first Champion, Ch. Adoram Dillypin Damon, he then went on to be awarded the Reserve in the Toy Group. Then again I remember in 1969 when Ch. Adoram Cinderfella of Pallas went Best in Show at LKA. What a thrill it was for him in those days, but he has made up so many Champions since then that the big ring cannot be quite so exciting – that is, unless you are an appointed judge, as he was when he had the honour of judging the Toy Group at Crufts, 1994, and the Utility Group there in 1995.

The prefix Adoram is well-known both here and abroad for the quality of Michael

Michael Quinney with BoB Ch. Dillypin Charlotte and judge Arthur Brown. City of Birmingham Canine Association Championship Show, 1979.

Photo: McFarlane.

Quinney's Pugs. Not all are bred by him, but they are usually sired by his stud dogs. He has campaigned and made up twelve English Champions and many overseas, and they have also passed on their good line to further generations. Ch. Harjen Merry Porthos of Adoram was often shown by Michael's friend, the late Terry MacHaffie. In 1983 Terry was awarded the MBE for his work as Chief Training Officer at the RAF Police Dog School, Nottingham.

Noelle Mackness has also bred some lovely Pugs, one being Michael Quinney's first Champion, Ch. Adoram Dillypin Damon, and another was Ch. Dillypin Charlotte. She also bred Ch. Phantasia of Paramin and Ch. Paramin Dillypin Pantaloon, who were owned and campaigned by Margo Raisin to gain their titles. Ch. Dillypin Delightful Doreen of Dobray, bred by Mrs Brady, was owned and campaigned by Noelle. Doreen was sired by Damon. Margo Raisin, one of our longest-established Pug breeders and exhibitors, has been a distinguished and loyal member of the Northern Pug Dog Club, having sat on their committee for a number of years. For some time she held the position of president. She has bred and owned many Champions. In the past she has exported a number of Pugs and passed on the 'Paramin' qualities to other countries. Ch. Patrick of Paramin, bred by Margo in 1967, was Nancy Tarbitt's first Champion. Other Paramin Champions were Ch. Patty of Paramin, Ch. Phanfare of Paramin of Dunlossit, Ch. Phauna of Paramin, Ch. Dolly Bird of Adoram and Ch. Paramin Polanaise of Hoonme.

HOONME, HYRCANIA AND SKEHANA

Alice Williams, a constant exhibitor during the sixties and seventies, made up four

Ch. Hyrcania Irish Imp. Owner/breeder Jean Manifold.   Photo: Diane Pearce.

Ch. Skehana Highland Laddie. Owner/ breeder Sue Welch.

Champions. Sadly in 1972 she had a dreadful disaster. A fire in her kennels caused her to lose twelve Pugs ranging from puppies to adults. Following this traumatic event, she became the proud owner of a young puppy, a gift from Margo Raisin. This puppy grew up to be Ch. Paramin Polanaise of Hoonme. Alice bred from Polanaise, who produced Ch. Hoonme Hansel.

When I first knew Jean Manifold she was a very excited exhibitor, having just made up a Champion, Ch. Hyrcania Afra. Afra was a beautiful Pug. No question about her colouring, she was pure apricot. Later came Ch. Hyrcania Irish Imp, a black. Another black who did a lot for the breed, although not a Champion, was Hyrcania Black Ferdy. He was the sire of Ch. Allt Hebe of Rosecoppice (owned by Eleanor English), Crufts' Best of Breed in 1978. Jean's last Champion and Group winner was Ch. Hyrcania Moonshine, a fawn.

Sue Welch, like myself, was first around during those times when it was tough to make up a Champion because the number of entries in Pug classes had reached their height. She told me quite recently that it took her fourteen years of breeding and showing, with many disappointments, before she had a Champion. That was Ch. Skehana Blackberry. Her sire was Rosecoppice Winstone of Neubraa. Winstone never did get his third ticket but proved himself a good stud dog. Sue has had a number of Champions since Blackberry – Ch. Skehana Highland Laddie, his daughter Ch. Skehana Jacqueline, another daughter from a different mating Ch. Skehana Hanah, and Ch. Skehana Heather of Ardglass, the latter owned by Theo Greenhill-Reid.

Ch. The Allt Hebe of Rosecoppice. Owner/breeder Eleanor English.

Ch. Pro Bono Pyebeta. Owner/breeder Pam Spencer-Beighton.

ROSECOPPICE AND PYEBETA

Eleanor English started showing and breeding fawns and made up Ch. Rosecoppice Tinkerbell as well as Ch. Phidgity Phiesta of Rosecoppice. Once Mrs Graham had introduced her to the black Pug, she has favoured those, especially after buying The Allt Hebe. She became Ch. The Allt Hebe of Rosecoppice and at Crufts in 1978 Eleanor was on top of the world when Hebe was made BOB and fifth in the Toy Group. When she was mated to Jean Manifold's Hyrcania Black Ferdy she produced John and Sylvia Smith's Ch.

Rosecoppice Blackjack. Blackjack became the sire of five Champions, including Colin and Jackie Smith's (no relation) Ch. Coljac Black Higgin. This was truly a good line of black breeding. Another black dog worthy of mentioning was Joyce Hargreave's Normpug Mark of Babraham who produced some good, winning stock, as did his son, Rosecoppice Winstone of Neubraa.

Pam Spencer-Beighton bred or owned about twelve Champions and her Pyebeta prefix is on the pedigrees of some lovely Pugs, both black and fawn. Her stud dog, Ch. Prendergast of Pyebeta, brought many successes. Prendergast sired five Champions including his son Ch. Pro Bono of Pyebeta. Pro Bono went Best in Show at LKA in 1968. He was the first Pug to win such a prestigious award since Ch. Banchory Lace in 1957. I can remember standing watching a crowd of photographers taking Pro Bono's photograph after his big win. While trying to get this little Pug's attention for a good picture, one photographer asked, "What do you call him?" There was a roar of laughter when Pam replied, "Jelly Boots." He received the Dog CC at Crufts in 1969 and was BOB in 1972.

Ch. Goodchance Eddystone. Bred by Ellen Brown. Owned by Norman Wooller.
Photo: Diane Pearce.

GOODCHANCE AND ANSAM

From Prendergast's mating to my own Goodchance Pharosa, daughter of Ch. Justatwerp of Cedarwood, I bred Ch. Goodchance Eddystone, owned and campaigned by Norman Wooller. Eddystone had two Champion sons and three Champion grandsons. His name has been handed down on many pedigrees. From the same litter as Eddystone came American Ch. Goodchance Sandetta owned by Ralph 'Buddy' Adair. The same litter also produced Goodchance Catherina. I kept Catherina and mated her to Ch. Eastonite Arthur of Elmsleigh. This mating produced Ch. Goodchance Medina. Medina was awarded seven CCs, including Crufts 1978 and seven Res. CCs. Sam and Joan Troth of the 'Ansam' prefix used Eddystone and had two lovely dogs from one litter. Ansam Xantie became a Champion, but his litter brother, Ansam Xavea, seemed to prefer the ladies to showing and he made a very good stud dog. He sired Ch. Pyenest Nicholas who has passed his qualities down to Neubraa and Clarique breeding.

Xavea was also the sire of Brian Bowden's

Ch. Goodchance Medina. Owner/breeder Ellen Brown.
Photo: Diane Pearce.

Ch. Ansam Xantie. Owner/breeder Sam and Joan Troth.
Photo: Garwood.

Ch. Rexdon Rubstic: The only Pug at that time to win two BIS at Championship Shows. Owner/breeder Brian Bowden.

Photo: Diane Pearce.

Ch. Goodchance Flower Power. Bred by Ellen Brown, owned by Joel Saffer.

Photo: David Dalton.

lovely Ch. Rexden Rubstic. Rubstic took twenty-seven CCs and eight Res. CCs. He was twice BIS at general Championship shows, namely Driffield in 1981 and Paignton in 1982, and Reserve BIS at Midland Counties in 1982. He was BIS at The Pug Dog Club Championship Show in 1982 and 1984, at its Open Show in 1982 and 1983, at the Northern Pug Dog Club Championship show in 1982 and the Scottish Pug Dog Club in the same year. This was truly a great achievement for a stunning dog.

Rubstic was the sire of my own Ch. Sneezwort Lily Langtry of Goodchance and Jenny Brown's (no relation) Ch. Sensayuma Silhouette. Silhouette mated to Ch. Hattella Wild Robin produced Ch. Sensayuma Paper Tiger. Tiger was mated to Ch. Sheffawn Shannigan and from this mating came Ch. Sensayuma Annabella to further this successful line of breeding for Jenny and Ian Brown. Annabella mated to Ch. Ardglass Noah produced Ch. Sensayuma Cotton Socks. That's what one calls successful breeding.

Ch. Hutzpah Harvest Moon of Ansam: Pug Dog record holder with 32 CCs. Bred by Mrs F. Cohen, owned by Sam and Joan Troth. Photo: David Dalton.

Ch. Sneezwort Lily Langtry of Goodchance. Bred by Beverley Purbrick. Owned by Ellen Brown.   Photo: Diane Pearce.

As well as breeding Ch. Ansam Xantie, Sam and Joan Troth have since bred two more Champions, Ch. Ansam Dantie and Ch. Ansam Beckie. As this book goes to press they are showing record-breaking Ch. Hutzpah Harvest Moon at Ansam who to date has collected 32 CCs. He was bred by Mr D. and Mrs F. Cohen.

IDE
Joe Braddon was known the world over as a judge and for his famous 'Bo-Pugs' of Ide. Joe had both fawns and blacks but I think he favoured the blacks. He owned many Champions including Bo-Jerk, Bo-Jiffy, Bo-Cassidy and Bo-Happy Man, all 'of Ide' and many more. Quite a number went overseas.

FLOCKTON AND SHURALAN
Dr and Mrs Ben Raven had a few Pugs in the early 1960s and bred three champion bitches in one litter sired by Ch. Adoram Dillypin Damon. Brenda Banbury showed and made up a number of Champions.

Pugs carrying her 'Flockton' prefix were exported and met with equal success. She has since concentrated on judging many other breeds both here and abroad. Miss Ella Clancy obtained her first Pug from Nancy Tarbitt and she became Ch. Nanchyl Gossamer. This was the first Champion that Nancy had bred. Ella and her friend, Rita Storey, have shown many Pugs, gaining top awards with Ch. Shuralan Aurelia and Ch. Shuralan Flavius.

CYRENE
Rene Meadows has owned and shown two Champions, Ch. Cyrene Penny Black and Ch. Cyrene Isa Black in Britain but she has also exported a number of successful Pugs, both black and fawn. She favours the blacks which carry the Babraham bloodline.

Cyrene Isa Minx. Owner/ breeder Rene Meadows.

Photo: Ernest T. Gasgoigne.

POLLYWOPS
Alison Mount owned Pugs many years before taking to the show ring and breeding, where she has since had a number of successes, making up three Champions. Her greatest joy was getting BOB at Crufts in 1993 with homebred Ch. Pollywops Master Angus, a fawn dog. Her

other two Champions were both blacks, Ch. Pollywops Miss Dulcie and her daughter, Ch. Pollywops Miss Millicent.

MAULICK

Monica Hopkinson has been breeding Pugs, both black and fawn, since 1964. Her first Champion that she bred was Ch. Maulick Aladdin, owned by Peter Newman. She has had many top prize-winning Pugs in recent years. Ch. Ronnor Roberta of Maulick, owned and campaigned by Monica, was bred by Mrs Tuck and sired by Ch. Goodchance Flower Power. Roberta won 7 CCs, 3 Res. CCs, many BOB at general Championship shows, a Toy Group and Res. Toy Group. She was the Bitch CC winner at Crufts 1993 and also 4th in the United Kingdom Toy Dog Society Top Toy Event in the same year. When mated to Pat Rufini's Ch. Pugini Prima Perfetta, Roberta produced a beautiful bitch, Ch. Maulick Upsy Daisy. She was Top Pug for 1995, has won 13 CCs, 9 Res. CCs, 5 BOB with Group placings plus BOB at Crufts 1996.

BELOW: Ch. Ronnor Roberta of Maulick. Bred by Mrs Tuck. Owned by Monica Hopkinson.

Ch. Pendlebury Lydia. Owner/breeder Mrs R Greenwell.
Photo: Russell Fine Art.

PENDLEBURY

Mrs R. Greenwell must be the UK's longest-established Pug breeder. For years she has shown Pugs of quality. Her very first Champion was Ch. Philip of Modelhouse in 1951. In 1969 Pendlebury Rockefella gained his title. He was owned and handled by the late Christine Bark, Mrs Greenwell's companion. In more recent years Mrs Greenwell has bred and handled Pendlebury Lydia to her title.

HATTELLA

Carol Kirk's first Champion was Hattella Wild Robin. He was a lovely show dog and also proved to be a good stud dog. Ch. Hattella Sea Pearl, Ch. Hattella Precious Pearl and Ch. Hattella The Duchess of Doghill were all successful bitches bred by her. Carol, together with her daughter Stella, is breeding and showing good stock. Their latest Champion, campaigned by Stella, is Ch. Hattella Captain Dibble.

ANMARRIC

Anne Bolton had a good run of Champion stud dogs through the 1980s to the 1990s. First came Ch. Anmarric Kingpin, then Ch.

Anmarric Alexandra. From these lines came Ch. Anmarric Inca. All proved to be good stud dogs.

RAGEMMA

Gail Saffer, who owns Boxers, became interested in Pugs in 1985 when she bought Goodchance Teddy Boy for her ten-year-old son, Joel. Little did she know what future it held for Joel. He showed Teddy Boy very successfully but wanted to aim higher. When my Ch. Sneezewort Lily Langtry of Goodchance had her second litter, Gail bought a bitch and the only dog in the litter, Goodchance Flower Power. Power was awarded his first CC in 1988 when James Cavallero from America judged at Bournemouth. He selected Flower Power from the Junior class. Joel, still quite young, now had the flaming ambition, "only the top will do". Success was growing. Flower Power became a Champion, collecting nine CCs and five Res. CCs. He was Res. Toy Group winner, Champion Stakes winner and BOB at Crufts 1990. Joel was then sixteen years of age. During those times there was also plenty of top winnings for Joel in the KCJO (this I have written about at the end of this chapter). Ch. Goodchance Flower Power was the sire of Joel's next Champion, Ch. Regencylodge Power Perfect, bred by Barbara Dabbs. He was also the sire of Ch. Ronnor Roberta of Maulick and Ch. Neutrino Anlic. Joel is now breeding under his own prefix 'Ragemma'.

REGENCYLODGE

Barbara Dabbs, breeder of Ch. Power Perfect is the daughter of one of the UK's long-standing breeders, Kathleen Haythornthwaite. They share the

Ch. Regencylodge Power Perfect. Bred by Barbara Dabbs. Owned by Joel Saffer.
Photo: Carol Ann Johnson.

'Regencylodge' prefix. Kathleen bred Ch. Spicy Boy of Regencylodge in 1969. This dog was owned and campaigned by Anita Edwards, one of England's top groomers.

NEUTRINO

The first Champion owned by Anne and Neville Collins and their son Chris was Ch.

Ch. Neutrino Anlic.
Owner/breeder Ann Collins.

Clemlee Spring Time, bred by Sylvia Clements. Then came Ch. Neutrino Anlic who followed his sire in becoming BOB at Crufts in 1991. Anlic was the Collins' first Pug to carry their own prefix 'Neutrino'. Many Neutrino Pugs are being shown today, usually amongst the prize-winners.

SMOOFAIR

There are two Sylvia Smiths in the breed which, at times, can become a little confusing. However, their husbands have different initials and, of course, they have different prefixes. Bernard and Sylvia Smith's 'Smoofair' Pugs have made quite a name for themselves. Sylvia owned a Pug many years before she started showing. When the time came to replace a much-loved pet Pug, she bought Donnadee Matilda Smoo from Mr and Mrs G. Coutts. Encouraged by the breeder and Monica Cummings, the owner of the stud dog Desperado of Doms, Sylvia decided to show Matilda. Much to her delight she gained her crown. The Smoofair family grew and grew and has been shown

successfully. Smoofair Wild Rose was BOB at Crufts in 1986 and her litter sister, Smoofair Willow Herb became a Champion.

PIZARRO

John and Sylvia Smith campaigned their first Pug, Cuckoohaven Pizarro, to gain his Championship title in 1978. He was followed by Ch. Rosecoppice Black Jack and then another black, Ch. Sheafdon Pal Joey at Pizarro. After these came two fawn bitches, Ch. Sheffawn Fair Sarah of Pizarro and Ch. Northside Starry-Eyes at Pizarro. None of these were homebred. John Smith has recently been appointed the Pug Dog Club's executive secretary.

BOURNLE

From their small kennel of Pugs, Mr and Mrs Les Elbourn have bred three English Champions, Ch. Bournle Isabel, Ch. Genevieve of Bournle and Ch. Bournle Ivanhoe. Bournle Belvedere of Cedarwood owned by Pauline Thorp proved a good stud dog. Some Bournle Pugs went abroad

Ch. Sheafdon Pal Joey at Pizarro, bred by Miss Haggie, and Ch. Sheffawn Fair Sarah of Pizarro, bred by Chris Baines. Both owned by John and Sylvia Smith.

Photo: Diane Pearce.

Ch. Bournle Isabel. Owner/breeder Elizabeth Elbourn.   Photo: Diane Pearce.

and were shown successfully, especially in America where Les and Elizabeth often visit and judge.

PUGNUS AND BENTWOOD
Eike Herold has had great successes with his Pugs having made a very sound start to his kennels by purchasing two lovely bitches, Cerne Chalumeau and Cerne Cymbal, from the late Chris Coleman. Eike campaigned them to their titles. These were

Ch. Bentwood Black Comedy. Owner/breeder the late Ian Fowler and Eike Herold.
Photo: Thomas Fall.

Ch. Ansadie Two with Pugnus. Bred by Miss S. King. Owned by Eike Herold.
Photo: Sally Ann Thompson.

to be followed by Ch. Pugnus Humoresque, Ch. Ardglass Theodora of Pugnus, Ch. Ansadie Two with Pugnus and Ch. Pugnus Olivia. Ch. Ansadie Two with Pugnus was twice BOB at Crufts, first in 1988 and again in 1989. With Eike's late partner Ian Fowler came some nice black Pugs, Ch. Bentwood Black Artemis, Ch. Bentwood Black Comedy and Bentwood Black Humbug.

MARRINAVALE
Kay and Pam Cooper have been breeding Pugs since 1967. They owned Two Pins Priority, the sire of Miss Wheeler's Ch. Thing Loo Agoo. 'Thing', as she was known, was very much a top prize-winner

in the seventies. The Cooper sisters' first Champion was Ch. Marrinavale Potty Dotty in 1980 and their latest is Ch. Marrinavale Mignonette.

CLARIQUE

I remember Andy Philbrick with her daughter Claire, then quite young, arriving at an Open show with a small puppy who wasn't at all happy with what she saw. Little did they think then that the puppy would become a Champion with many successes. Ch. Neubraa Miranda was the pride of the Philbrick family. Another success followed – Berrymul Candytuft got her title also. Then, carrying their own prefix for the first time, came Ch. Clarique Unique. He received a CC at Crufts in 1992. Mated to my own Goodchance Magnolia he produced Goodchance Camellia and Goodchance Little Rosa. Camellia, handled by my granddaughter, Rebecca, has been showing quite successfully, gaining to date one CC and four Res CCs. Her litter sister, our miracle baby, Rosa, has been shown by Rebecca's sister, Angela.

Ch. Clarique Unique. Owner/breeder Andy and Claire Philbrick.

PALLYN AND POOSBURY

When Linda Bissell mated her bitch, The Pig of Pallyn, to Doreen Davies' Poosbury Sweet William in 1983 there started a good line of breeding for both these ladies. That mating produced two Champions in the one litter. A dog, Ch. Pallyn Piggy Bank was bought as a puppy by Jean Lockett. He was her first Pug. He showed his qualities when he first stepped into the ring and I was pleased to award him his first CC coming from the Junior class at the PDC's Championship Show in 1985. In 1987 he was BOB at Crufts. Linda Bissell kept Piggy Bank's litter sister, Pallyn Piglet, and she too became a Champion. From then on both Linda and Jean have bred some lovely Pugs. Linda bred Ch. Pallyn Pigture of Jansara, owned and campaigned by Sarah James, and Ch. Pallyn Paddington Bear, owned by Mrs Jordan.

Doreen Davies had more successes with Sweet William as a stud dog and later added other stud dogs of her own breeding to her small kennel, namely Poosbury Piggy Malone, Poosbury Charlie Farley and Ch. Poosbury Punch Drunk who was previously owned and campaigned to his title by Mr Sprason. Between them these dogs have produced Champions and numerous lovely Pugs. Doreen does not show her Pugs very often but prefers to be at home with her puppies. She has exported quite a few Pugs with equal success and the name of Poosbury has become well-known in the Pug world.

SNEEZWORT

Beverley Purbrick bought Goodchance Edwina as a pet from me. She decided to breed from her and used Ch. Cedarwood Willopop Isa Wonderboy. The mating produced Sneezwort Tufry Tufnut. He sired one Champion, Ch. Rapsody of Beaverdale, owned by Sheila Armstrong. When my own Ch. Sneezwort Lily Langtry of Goodchance was mated to Sneezwort Tufry Tufnut, from the litter of five was Goodchance Flirty Bertie of Sneezwort. He in turn was the sire of Ch. Sneezwort Raven, a black bitch. Goodchance Flirty Bertie was later exported to Sweden. Bertie's litter sister, my own Goodchance Victoria, received two CCs and three Res. CCs. Sneezwort Pugs have continued with success from this early start.

CLAYBRIDGE

Mr and Mrs Saycell made up their first Pug Champion, Ch. Claybridge Beauty, in 1983. Since then they have bred seven Champions including Ch. Claybridge Call Me Syril, owned by Rosemary Bradburn (the PDC's *Bulletin* Editor). Syril was often handled by Mrs Saycell, his breeder. Rosemary also owned Ch. Paramin Pioneer bred by Margo Raisin. Mrs Saycell also bred Ch. Claybridge I'm Dian, owned and campaigned by Mrs Coates.

SHEFFAWN

Chris Baines has bred some lovely Pugs, both black and fawn, including Ch. Sheffawn Ginger Punch in 1980. Her present day Champion is Ch. Sheffawn Shannigan. She also bred Ch. Sheffawn She's Wilma of Jansara, owned by Sarah Hayward (nee James) and Ch. Sheffawn Fair Sara of Pizarro, owned by John and Sylvia Smith.

JUSTABUL

Mr and Mrs Boyes have had some successful breeding, making up three Champions – Ch. Justabul Bartram, Ch. Justabul Angelica and Ch. Justabul Camela.

PILLETTE

Jean Pearce bred and showed some lovely Pugs during the 1970s and 1980s. Ch. Pillette Perhaps So, Ch. Pillette Priority and Ch. Pillette Penny Princess all gained their titles.

ALWIL

Mr and Mrs W. Burrows owned four Champions, three of which were homebred, Ch. Alwil Angela, Ch. Alwil Devil Woman and Ch. Alwil Thomas Plunkett. Ch. Willopops Mopsie of Alwil was bred by Jean Young.

RUBATUM AND BARRYANN

Mr and Mrs T. Hilder owned three champions, Ch. Bo Filbert of Ide, Ch. Moeno's Minstral and Ch. Barryann Bizzy Body of Rubatum. Mr Hilder was chairman

Ch. Master Edward of Barryann. Owner/breeder Mr and Mrs B. P. Welham.

Photo: Tom Hilder.

of the NPDC for many years and Mrs Hilder was at one time editor of *The Lead*, the NPDC's own Bulletin.

Mr and Mrs B. Welham have had a number of successes with their Pugs, both black and fawn. They bred and campaigned Ch. Barryann Master Edwards to his title, being awarded three CCs and two Res. CCs. He sired three Champions. They also bred Ch. Barryann El Sid, owned by Marion Wright. Both of these dogs were fawn. Mr and Mrs Welham had further success with blacks, once breeding two Champions in one litter. These were Ch. Barryann Barnaby and Ch. Barryann Bizzy Body of Rubatum. Barnaby was awarded seven CCs and five Res. CCs.

TIDEMILL

Nigel Marsh and his partner Terry Purse have had quite a few successes with their Pugs over the last few years. In 1995 they were delighted to make up Ch. Simos Delia's Delight Tidemill. Terry is currently show secretary for the PDC. Allan Pritchard owns the last male black Pug to gain his title since 1989. Ch. Xenos Black

He's Tobias of Pagan, owned and campaigned by Allan, was bred by Kathy Newsome.

FFAIN

June Martin started showing Pugs in 1991 and has successfully bred two Champions, Ch. Ffain Miss Rosa Dartle and Ch. Ffain Devilline of Nanchyl, owned by Nancy Tarbitt. There are other very nice Ffain Pugs being shown.

NANCHYL

Nancy Tarbitt, as everyone who owns a Pug knows, must be England's most successful Pug breeder. Since the mid-1960s, when she first started to show Pugs, up to the present day, she has owned or bred seventeen Champions, all from her own line of breeding. She holds the record for the bitch winning the most CCs and I am sure I am right in saying that her Pugs have won more BOBs than anyone else's. Her Crufts record from 1978 to 1992 consists of 10 CCs with six of her Pugs, taking five BOBs, one Group and one Res. Group. Her line of breeding not only

Ch. Simos Delia's Delight Tidemill. Bred by Mrs C. K. Agrell. Owned by Terry Purse and Nigel Marsh.   Photo: Carol Ann Johnson.

Ch. Nanchyl Xerxes. Owner/breeder Nancy Tarbitt.

Photo: McFarlane.

Ch. Rosalia of Nanchyl: Present-day CC record holder. Bred by Mrs Reynolds, owned by Nancy Tarbitt.   Photo: David Dalton.

produces good, sound bitches but dogs as well. When used at stud these dogs have been useful in passing on their excellent qualities. To go through all Nancy's successful Pugs and their breeding lines would need a chapter of its own, so I will just highlight a few. Her first Champion, Ch. Patrick of Paramin, was bred by Margo Raisin and this was the start of a long line of Champions. Patrick sired six Champions. In particular, when he was mated to Nanchyl Lynfield Amber, bred by Nancy, they produced Ch. Nanchyl Gossamer and Ch. Nanchyl Imp from two different litters. They both received their crown within ten days of each other. From then on Nancy appears to have had one Champion after another, always keeping to her own line of breeding. Ch. Nanchyl Roxanna came into the ring in 1977, and she swept the board by becoming the bitch record holder with 32 CCs. Roxanna's son, Ch. Nanchyl Xerxes, soon followed in his mother's footsteps, winning 27 CCs. He was BOB and Reserve in the Toy Group at Crufts 1984. He proved to be a good stud dog, siring seven English Champions and one American Champion. More Champions were produced from the Nanchyl kennels.

Another one who proved to be an excellent stud dog was Ch. Nanchyl Zechim. He sired eight English Champions and one Swedish and International Champion. His most successful offspring was produced when he was mated to an outcross bitch. The outcome was Ch. Rosalia of Nanchyl who took the record for winning the most CCs away from her great-grandmother, Roxanna. In 1992 she was BOB and won the Toy Group at Crufts. Coming up to the present day, Nancy has Ch. Ffain Devilline of Nanchyl, sired by her own Ch. Nanchyl Zechim. This record is certainly something to be proud of.

In this chapter I have tried to include many of the current top Pugs and their breeders. Please forgive me if anyone is disappointed about not being mentioned. This would have been just an oversight – no other reason.

JUNIOR HANDLERS

I cannot conclude without a word about junior members, for they are the future of the Pug in Britain. Furthermore, our breed is fortunate enough to have some of the top juniors in Britain. Those that I mention have all been members of the Kennel Club Junior Organisation and the Junior Handling Association. The KCJO involves juniors in many aspects of dogs, in particular the KCJO Stakes Class held at Championship Shows which is judged on the dog's merit. The JHA is specifically for handling only.

Samantha Sarl did a lot of winning in Junior Handling from a very early age. In the 1988 Semi-finals of the JHA, which is always held at Richmond Championship show, Samantha won the 6 to 11 year class. This qualified her to attend the Pedigree Chum Finals in 1989. At the 1990 JHA

ABOVE: Melina Matlock with Toadabode Grumbling Gwenny.

RIGHT: Joel Saffer with Ch. Goodchance Flower Power.

Semi-finals, Samantha took second prize with a borrowed Pug. Her own Pug had unfortunately been stung by a wasp.

Melina Matlock was another top prize winner in handling classes. She came fifth at the 1988 JHA Semi-finals and fourth in 1989. In 1990 she won the 12 to 16 years class and qualified for the Pedigree Chum Finals in 1991. At the Welsh Kennel Club Championship Show she took first prize in the KCJO Stakes Class which qualified her for Crufts where she came fifth in the Toy Group Stakes. Melina is now breeding and campaigning her own dogs under her own prefix 'Misstoad'.

In 1986, when Joel Saffer was twelve years old, he qualified his first Pug, Goodchance Teddy Boy, in numerous KCJO Stakes Classes. This took him to

Crufts in 1987 where he won the Toy Group Stakes. It was the first year that this event was held. At the time Joel won he said "It was a fantastic feeling, walking in the big ring. I would like to do it again, preferably in the breed." Well, Joel did just that. In 1990 his Ch. Goodchance Flower Power got BOB at Crufts. Joel was then 16 years old. 1991 saw him again in the big ring at Crufts when he won the KCJO Toy Stakes and then went on to become the overall KCJO Stakes Winner. From when he was ten years old, Joel has had numerous wins showing his Pugs in the breed and KCJO Stakes Classes where he has been successful in qualifying three different Pugs. In the JHA Semi-finals in 1989 he was placed fifth and in 1990 and 1991 he was third. He is now judging and

Angela Naylor with Goodchance Little Rosa. Best Junior Handler, Welsh Kennel Club Championship Show, 1993.

Photo: Alan V. Walker

breeding under his own prefix 'Ragemma'.

My own granddaughters, Rebecca and Angela Naylor, have been involved with Pugs since 1988 when they both became members of the KCJO and JHA. Their interest was strengthened in 1991 when they took to the show ring with their own

Dean Stead with Pallyn Pig 'N' Whistle of Ansam, 1990.

Pugs. Rebecca, now my 'Goodchance' partner, has shown Goodchance Camellia to gain many awards. In 1993 she won two KCJO Stakes Classes with qualifications for Crufts 1994 where she won the Toy Group Stakes and went on to the big ring to become the reserve overall winner. In 1994 she won five KCJO Stake Classes, qualifying for Crufts in 1995. Once again she was in the final line-up. After qualifying six times during 1995 for Crufts 1996 Rebecca was unable to take part because I was judging the breed and am joint owner of Camellia. At the JHA Semi-finals she took fourth place in 1993, third place in 1994 and second place in 1995. She has had many successes at Open and Championship Shows and is now judging the breed at Open shows and Junior Handling classes at Open and Championship show level.

Angela has done well with Goodchance Little Rosa in breed classes, including BOB at Open shows. In Junior Handling Angela has won first prize in classes at numerous Open and Championship shows. She has

Rebecca Naylor with Goodchance Camellia: Winner of the Toy Group in the KCJO Stakes and Reserve overall winner, Crufts 1994.

qualified every year for the JHA Semifinals at Richmond where she has succeeded in getting in the final line-up. In the 1996 semi-finals she handled her sister's Pug, Goodchance Camellia, and took second place out of a class of thirty-three juniors in the 12 to 16 years age group. In 1995 Angela and Rosa were at Crufts on all four days demonstrating for the Good Citizen Dog Scheme, where Rosa passed her test and received her certificate.

Stella Kirk shows her mother's 'Hatella' Pugs to gain top awards and has recently made up a Champion. Adele Bowie did a lot of winning during her days in Junior competitions and has also campaigned her home-bred Pug to gain his title. Dean Stead has handled Pugs since he was very young and qualified for the JHA Semifinals at Richmond. A few years ago, when he was seriously ill in hospital, causing much anxiety to his family, his grandparents, Sam and Joan Troth, promised him a lovely Pug to show when he was well. When the crisis was over Dean was given Pallyn Pig 'N' Whistle of Ansam, who helped his recovery. This little dog won one CC and a Res. CC. Dean is now breeding under his own prefix 'Dejosa'.

These youngsters are now teenagers and adults, but they have already had many years showing and handling their Pugs with top successes. The years they spent with the KCJO and JHA have served as an apprenticeship for their future. We are very fortunate to have young people like these interested in the Pug.

PUG DOGS CLUBS IN BRITAIN
THE PUG DOG CLUB

It was in *The Stockman*, 1881, that the idea of a Pug Dog Club was first discussed and it was finalised with the Kennel Club in 1883. The Pug Dog Club was one of the earliest clubs to be registered at the KC. Mr James W. Berrie was the first president and Admiral Sir George Giffard KCB and Lady Giffard were vice-presidents. The honorary secretary was Miss M.A.E. Holdsworth. Incidentally, she was the first lady ever to judge at a Dog Show. This was at the Maidstone Show in 1886. The PDC's first show was held in 1885. The third annual show in 1887 was run by Charles Cruft who was by then secretary of the Club. It is said that through promoting shows for the PDC, together with those of the Toy Spaniel, Collie and Terrier Clubs, he became known as a promoter.

There were sixty-six Pugs entered in the Kennel Club's first Stud Book in 1874 when entries at shows were between 130 and 150. Pugs were quite popular. In the early 1900s another club was formed, namely the London and Provincial Pug Dog Club but it did not meet with success. An extract from *Our Dogs* of December 24th 1926 stated that "All the formalities for the amalgamation of the Pug Dog Club and the London and Provincial Pug Dog Club having been completed, the two clubs have now joined forces and will in future be known as The Pug Dog Club". The membership fee in 1883 was one guinea (£1.05 or approximately $1.50) and, unbelievably, remained unaltered until 1973, two years after decimalisation of the British currency, when it was increased to £1.50 ($2.25). As with the current trend it has risen frequently since then. At the time of going to press the fee for British members is £6 ($9.00) and for overseas members it is £8 ($12). Membership of the Club is forever increasing. Today there are 650 British members and more than 100 overseas members.

The Club runs three show a year, a Championship Show, an Open Show and a Limit Show. Each year a garden party is held during the summer and seminars and matches are arranged from time to time. Members receive a free Club *Bulletin* four times a year and are at liberty to write to the editor with any news of interest for publication. A spoon is awarded to all CC winners during the year provided the judge is on the Club's judging list. A new Club Handbook is produced every five years.

The Club has an abundance of silver cups and trophies. Some are of great value, dating back to the 1800s. When Lou Green (Harloo) took over as cup steward some time after World War II she discovered that many of them were missing. The committee decided to make a claim with the insurance company for the losses, but it was agreed to first contact the jewellers who were responsible for valuing them. Major Gibson, who was secretary at the time, wrote to the firm, who replied saying that they had some of the trophies in their possession and could someone identify them. Major Gibson and Mrs Green were delegated to visit the strong room of The Crown Jewellers, Garrard & Co. Ltd., London where they were surprised and delighted to find many trophies belonging to the PDC. In the end they were all found, according to records. They had been put away during the war years. The Finsbury Major Bowl (for Best Dog in Show at the Championship Show) and the Boscobel Golden Bowl (for BIS at the Open Show), both of which are now over 100 years old, were two of the missing cups that were retrieved.

The committee of the PDC consists of ten members excluding ex-officio members who have no power to vote. The ex-officio members are the president, the executive secretary, the show secretary and the treasurer. The president and the committee members serve for three years. The longest serving committee members resign each year and are replaced by newly elected members. Regardless of the committee's three-year term, they do have to come up for re-election each year. All rules must be carried out according to the PDC Rule Book and the KC.

Pugs have had their full share of rising and falling popularity, as previously stated, but they have always remained a good steady breed because of loyal breeders. At the turn of the century the registration of Pugs at the KC was improving. The years went by, with two wars intervening, but Pug breeders continued regardless. In 1945 at the end of the Second World War there were 111 Pugs registered. The following year there were 163. Each year the number increased until, as has been mentioned, it reached its summit in 1962 with 1,668 Pugs being registered. From then on it has gradually made a decline and at the last count in 1995 there were 519 Pugs registered. There are some beautiful Pugs in the ring today and many good and caring breeders, but sad to say there are others who could do better in the way they treat their Pugs. Breeding, just to sell, regardless of where the dogs go, was not meant for this lovely, aristocratic breed of dog. Pugs have always been special and still are. We must not spoil the breed in ways detrimental to its structure and character.

THE NORTHERN PUG DOG CLUB
The Northern Pug Dog Club was first started in 1911 but had a very bad beginning with the 1914 War following so soon. Harry Green made an effort to re-start it in 1927 but lacked support and it

was dissolved two years later. Again in 1939 it was discussed with all good intentions but once more a war interrupted the proceedings.

Talks about the Club were reconvened in 1949 and the NPDC was able to make a fresh and successful start. A committee was formed and a meeting was held in Blackburn to formulate a book of rules. News to members was typed out by Mrs Grimshaw on an old typewriter. A number of committee meetings took place to get things moving. It was several years before the NPDC had a sufficiently sound financial position to hold a show of its own. A number of present-day breeders remember those early days. A 56 Class Open Show was held in 1956 at the Leeds Corn Exchange incorporating four other Toy Breed Clubs. BOB was Alice Laver's Alava Victory Roll who went on to be BIS. At a later date Victory Roll gained his title. In 1960 the Club held its first Championship Show and from then on the NPDC has successfully run Championship, Open and Limited Shows annually.

THE SCOTTISH PUG DOG CLUB
Pugs also have a Scottish Club. A meeting was held in the Caledonian Hotel, Edinburgh, on February 2nd 1925, to inaugurate the Club. It was proposed by Mrs C.J. Wilson and seconded by Mrs R. Watt that the Scottish Pug Dog Club be instituted and an application be made to the Scottish Kennel Club for registration and title. This was carried through and the Club ran favourably until 1939. No meetings were held during the war years and there seem to be no records of the Club again until February 5th 1947 when Miss E. McNair was elected as president. A report on the Club in 1952 states: "One

Open Show is held annually where various cups are put up. They also support the Scottish Kennel Club Show and English Championship Show and other shows in the North. The Club issues a news-sheet to members." In 1962 Mrs Theo Greenhill-Reid became secretary and treasurer of the Scottish PDC, the position she still holds today. In 1972 the Club was granted Championship status and ran their first Championship Show. It now runs a Championship and an Open Show annually.

THE WALES AND WEST OF ENGLAND PUG DOG CLUB

In 1986 Pug breeders in Wales felt that they also needed their own Club. A meeting was held and an application sent to the Kennel Club asking for permission to form the Welsh Pug Dog Club. This was turned down by the KC who stated that there were not enough Welsh breeders forming the membership and suggested that they change the name. Consequently the name was changed to the Wales and West of England Pug Dog Club and permission was granted in 1988. Rules of the Club state that thirteen members sit on the committee of which three shall reside in the West of England and ten in Wales. Championship Show status was given to hold their first Championship Show with CCs in 1994 and their second in 1995. Both were very successful shows. However, in 1994 the KC decided to cut down on shows awarding CCs in 1996 and unfortunately the Wales and West of England PDC became one of the victims. The Club has since heard that they have been granted CCs for 1997. Let's hope this will continue. The Club has now organised a Pug rescue service.

THE PUG DOG WELFARE ASSOCIATION

The breed also has an excellent welfare known as The Pug Dog Welfare Association, Registered Charity Number 276067. Great care is taken of any Pug in need of a home whether unwanted, neglected or through unfortunate circumstances. It was in 1972 that Monica Cummings and Mildred Inge felt that there was a need for such a society. When they put the idea to the committee and members of the PDC it was met with great approval. They were joined by Ena Tullett and Sue Welch and the scheme was started. At later dates Jean Manifold, Vivien Dudley, Margaret Statham, Ella Clancey and Theo Greenhill-Reid also became trustees.

As soon as there is news of a Pug needing a home, arrangements are made for the orphan to be collected from whatever part of the country necessary. The Pug is seen by a vet and, if there are any problems, is attended to until fit and well enough to go to a new home. Many bitches are spayed. Adopted homes are vetted before the Pug is passed over. No papers, such as pedigree and names of previous owners, go with the Pug. Naturally money is needed to run the association and this is raised by donations, legacies and various other methods. In 1974 Ena Tullet, with the help of Sue Welch, organised a party in her own garden at East Grinstead, Sussex, to raise money for Pug Dog rescue. This was so successful that, after four years, its popularity had outgrown Ena's garden and it was moved to a cricket ground and pavilion in Lingfield, Surrey. Now, every year a PDWA garden party is held, with many stalls, raffles, tombolas and auctions raising money to help finances. To add to the enjoyment of the day, games are organised for both owners and Pugs. Highlights of this event are Pug races, a fancy dress (for the Pugs of course!) and a grand parade of Pugs adopted through the Welfare with their very proud and happy owners. This is indeed a most enjoyable day for everyone and the profit made usually reaches four figures, which is a great help towards the running of the association. As we all know, vet fees and petrol costs are very high, so the funds raised are put to good use.

One rescue case was when a call came that a Pug had been run over. Three to four hours were spent chasing around trying to find the Pug. The first enquiry was at a Public House, where it was said that the Pug was in the hands of a vet. The vet passed the Pug on to the Police. The Police said that they had sent the Pug to a Dogs Home. The Dogs Home said that they could not let the dog go, the Pug must remain at the Dog's Home for one week in case the owner made a claim. When the week was up, no claim had been made and the Pug was collected. My goodness me! I've never seen anything like it. At a guess the bitch was about seven years of age. She weighed only seven pounds, had one eye, a wry mouth with a hanging tongue and a hernia the size of a tennis ball, with no exaggeration. She really was a bad sight. The Welfare requested that she saw a vet and all expenses would be paid from their funds. "Minnie" was operated on. Two hernias were removed and a hysterectomy performed. This was followed by a number of visits to the vet with small problems before she was discharged at a cost of £313. All expenses were paid by the Welfare. Faye Cutler, who had nursed her with loving care through all her problems, became so fond of her that she decided to keep her as a companion for her already adopted Pug, Jason. A happy end to a sad story. The vet's comment was, "You are a very lucky dog!" Not all cases are as bad as this, although many of these Pugs have problems, but nothing is too much trouble for the Welfare to deal with.

11 *PUGS WORLDWIDE*

M any more people travel overseas attending dog shows today than they did in my early days but we are all brought closer together, united in our love of this little dog. It is for this reason that I feel it is necessary to include in my book a brief outline of shows and showing in some other countries, so that one knows what to expect as a visitor. I have also included a short history of the Pug in some of these selected countries.

AUSTRALIA

Pugs have been in South Australia for well over a hundred years. They probably arrived with wealthy immigrants, since the Pug was at a peak in its popularity in England during the reign of Queen Victoria, but there are no records to say exactly where they landed. Some people were helped by masters of vessels, like Captain Wagstaff of *La Hogue*, a London-registered migrant and cargo ship. In 1878 Captain Wagstaff imported Romeo and Juliet for E.F. Steven of Pitt Street, Sydney. A year later, Mr Steven imported Judy, a sister of Tumtum. They were from Max (Punch) ex Vic. Vic was a daughter of Click, the son of Lamb and Moss, two

Chineses Pugs that arrived in England from Peking in 1860. We read so much about them in Pug history as being the forefathers of the breed in England.

From Australian research, the first record of Pugs shown in New South Wales was in the Agricultural Society catalogue in 1870. Just two Pugs were entered, but no names were given. At a later date five or six were entered. As with English registration at that time, only pet names were used. As my informant remarked: "Over a period, 'Bob' was a prominent sire, and if it was the same 'Bob' on each occasion, he must have been a busy little body."

At the end of the nineteenth century coat colouring was mentioned as 'Apricot and Fawn', 'Grey and Black', 'Fawn and Black Points' and 'Silver and Grey'. Names of breeders were becoming known and they were using prefixes and suffixes. Mrs Classon, prefix Sunlight, had by 1908 bred four Champions, all apricot fawns. By 1910, blacks were becoming popular and in 1913 classes were allocated for blacks only, and they outnumbered all other colours. In 1911, Mrs Shepherd imported from England a Champion called Master Speedwell, bred by Miss Woolridge, and also Champion Princess Dombey. These Pugs were used successfully and Mrs Shepherd kept Speedwell as her prefix.

Some kennels based in the Victoria area were also established from English imports. In the 1930s Mrs Catteral (Winton) obtained her Pugs from Mrs Swainston Goodger. Mr C. Thompson established his Leprenas kennels from Miss A. Gretton (Hazelbridge) and Miss M. Masland (Masbeck). Other English breeders who helped to establish good stock in Australia were Mrs Bancroft-Wilson (Longlands), Mr G.W. Kerrod (Hopworth), and Mrs Wendy Allen (Goldengleam). These were the early pioneers. Mrs Tovey (Drayton), Mrs Brooks (Corrard), Mrs York (Mons) and Mrs Slight (Europaka) dominated the breed in the early 1930s with blacks and fawns. There was also E. Nicholson (Hayilah), Miss A. Coulter (Ortona), whose kennels produced several Grand Champions, E. Kennedy (Norfolk), Miss Warner and L. Erickson (Creston), with his kennels of blacks and fawns. All these kennels were producing good stock prior to World War II.

In 1947, after the war, there was a rapid build-up of Pugs and many more kennels were established. Transport was being made easier, including the rapid expansion of air travel and private ownership of motor vehicles. A large number of breeders were now able to exhibit in breed and major shows in other states, especially Victoria and South Australia. Thus, with new-found friends, there was an interchange of ideas and clubs were beginning to form. At the same time there was a surge of imports from the United Kingdom and later from New Zealand. Their lines can be traced in most of today's pedigrees. All this resulted in entries of around 100 Pugs at the Sidney

Australian Ch. Patrian Chaucer carries UK breeding.
Owner/breeder/handler Patsy Muirden.

Royals in the early 1950s.

In the 1950s other prefixes such as Cobby, Bataan and Aureate were having a marked effect on the breed and formed a base for the Auriole, Boorooma and Tonlea kennels. By now Australia was becoming independent and established in breeding. May 1949 saw the inauguration of the Australian Pug Dog Club and in 1955 the Pug Dog Club of Victoria was formed. In the late 1950s and early 1960s there were two outstanding stud and show dogs, namely Leer and Hart's Masgay Majestic and Aureate China Son bred by Mrs H. Chew and owned by Mrs G. Lord, who

Australian Ch. Patrian Seashell. Owner/breeder/handler Patsy Muirden.

had just founded her 'Tengwah' Kennels.

In 1966, the 'Aureate' prefix was bequeathed to Mrs D. Alexander. Ray Alexander, in partnership with his mother, Dot, is another successful breeder who has had some lovely Pugs. He has used Pugs imported from England, some with my own breeding. A few years ago he successfully reared a litter of ten puppies. Probably the most successful breeder in Australia is Patsy Muirden, for during her forty years in Pugs, Patsy has bred or owned forty Champions. She is at present showing Australian Ch. Patrian Seashell and Ch. Patrian Chaucer. Chaucer is by Ch. Jeni Wren of Suepar (UK import) and Australian Ch. Patrian Conrad (now in the USA). Conrad's sire and dam lines are also from UK stock.

Mrs P.V. Lambert had successes with two top Pugs in 1992, namely Australian Ch. Upsandowns Simon and Australian Ch. Upsandowns Lotus. Others from 'down under' currently showing and breeding Pugs with success are Alison Su with her 'Regal' Pugs, L. and S. R. Heidenreich with 'Mopsorden' Pugs, Mrs J. O. Longley (Leelong), Ben J. Luxton (Obsidion), Jock and Elaine McRae (Birsay), Verna Wright (Gailyn), John and Jessamy Morrissey (Pugalugs), Esme Stringer (Gilgai), Norm Downey (Westcourt) and Mrs M. Cochrane. Bonny Richardson is the historian of the Pug Dog Club of New South Wales. Although she is no longer breeding, she retains her love of, and interest in, Pugs.

1994 was a special year for the Pug Club of Victoria Inc. They celebrated their Ruby Anniversary. A Championship Show was held at the Royal Showgrounds, Ascot Vale, and they were delighted to welcome as their judge Mrs Lorene Vickers-Smith from the USA. It was a most successful show, with lots of trophies and sashes on offer by generous donors. The Best Pug at this prestigious show was the dog, Ch. Gilgai Jet Son, bred by the Gilgai Kennels and owned by K.M. Mahood. Runner-up was Pugini Piero at Poosbury (UK import) bred by Pat Rufini and owned by the Gailyn Kennels.

Rules and regulations regarding exhibition in South Australia are governed

128

Aust. Ch. Upsandowns Lotus.
Bred by Mr A. Morris. Owned by Mr. V. P.
Lambert.

Mopsorden Hei Brontie.
Bred by L. and S. R. Heidenreich. Owned
by Jennifer Horan.

by the South Australian Canine Association. The Breed Standard is taken exactly from the Standard as set out by the Kennel Club of England. There are seven Groups: (1) Toys, (2) Terriers, (3) Gundogs, (4) Hounds, (5) Working Dogs, (6) Utility and (7) Non-Sporting. All the breeds in the Toy Group are the same as in the UK apart from the addition of the Tibetan Spaniel. All classes in the Group are given awards. The classes are Best Baby, Minor, Puppy, Junior, Intermediate, Australian Bred and Open. Novice, Graduate and Limit are rarely used by Clubs these days. In each class there are three class placings, given from left to right. Only when there are large numbers of entries in classes at a Royal or Breed Specialty Show are up to five places awarded. The winner of each class goes forward for each Best of Class in Show, against all the other Group Class winners. The Best in Group is chosen from all the Best of Breeds of a Group and then the Runner-Up to that Breed comes into the ring and the judge selects a Runner-Up in Group. The winner of Best In Show is

chosen from the seven Best in Group winners and it is automatically Best In Show of the Class in which it was entered. A Runner-Up In Show is selected from the remaining Group winners and the Runner-Up in the Group from which the BIS came.

Making up a Champion in Australia is quite different from in the UK, because the number of entries in most breeds does not come anywhere near the numbers seen in Britain. The judge awards a CC for each sex of a breed. A CC may be withheld if the judge considers that the exhibits are not up to the Breed Standard. 100 points are required for a Championship title. Each CC consists of five points plus one point for each exhibit of the sex present and shown, up to a maximum of 25 points in any one show. In a rare breed where there is only one exhibit, six points are gained for a CC. Thus for these breeds it takes seventeen CCs to make up a Champion. The points gained at breed level are cancelled if the exhibit wins Best in Group at the show, as this is worth 25 points. Therefore four Best in Group awards would make a Champion, providing that these are awarded by not less

*Aureate Aramis.
Owned by Ray
Alexander.*

than four different judges. Points are only allotted to exhibits six months of age or over that are exhibited in an ordinary class. At All Breeds and Group Shows judges reports are not published in the dog papers because they are not compulsory. A Breed Specialty Club may ask a judge to give a critique to be printed in a Club newsletter.

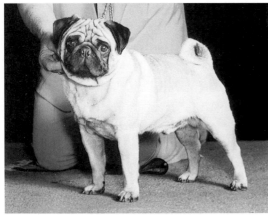

*Australian Ch. Leelong Coxwain.
Owner/breeder Mrs J.O. Longley.*

EIRE
The Irish Kennel Club is the governing body for dogs and dogs shows in Eire. In 1995 the IKC was honoured to host the World Conference of Kennel Clubs. The most important show organised by the IKC is the St. Patrick's Day Championship Show and in 1995 it drew a record 2681 dogs. Licences for any dog event in Eire will only be granted to organisations affiliated to the IKC. In 1994 there were 21 All Breed Championship shows, 8 Group Shows and 115 Breed Championship shows plus Open and Limited shows dealt with by the IKC. All dogs and bitches entered for shows in Eire must be registered with the IKC. The people of Eire have their own Irish Pug Dog Club but as far as I know they do not run a show of their own. The Breed Standard for the Pug in Eire is the same as the one published by the English KC.

At a Championship show there can be seven different classes in a breed and separate classes for dogs and bitches. Briefly, the classes are Minor Puppy (6 to 9 months), Puppy (6 to 12 months), Junior (6 to 18 months), Novice (not having won a Green Star, a CC or two first prizes in classes lower than this one), Graduate (not having won five first prizes in Open, Limit or Graduate classes at a show where Green stars are awarded or 23 points in the Green Star competition or a CC), Limit (having won eight first prizes in Open or Limit Classes or 38 Green Star points or 2 CCs) and the Open Class (all dogs/bitches).

More details can be found in the catalogues of the shows. At the St. Patrick's Day Championship show in 1996 there were eight classes for Pugs, namely Puppy, Junior, Graduate and Open Classes for dogs and for bitches. Placings and prize cards are given to the First, Second, Third and Reserve in each class. The route to becoming the Best in Show is as in Shows licensed by the English Kennel Club. However, in Eire, there are seven groups. They are Hound, Gundog, Terrier, Utility, Working, Pastoral and Toy. Hence the Toy Group is slightly different to that of the English KC. There are also Junior Handling Classes divided into three groups according to age. They are Group 1 (10 to 12 years), Group 2 (13 to 15 years) and Group 3 (16 to 18 years).

The Green Star system was adopted in Eire in 1978. An index figure is allocated to each sex, also to mixed dog and bitch classes in each breed. It is arrived at by dividing the total number of valid exhibits at a Championship show by the number of Shows at which Green Stars were offered in that breed during the previous year. Where the total number of exhibits actually shown is equal to the index figure, the five Green Star points will be awarded. Points are added and deducted according to a percentage above and below that figure but no award will be less than one point, or greater than ten points, and no breed is allocated an index figure less than five. Before a dog or bitch can become a Champion he or she must win a total of not less than forty Green Star points including one of the following: winning four lots of five points in the breed under four different judges or winning two lots of five points and one lot of ten points in the breed under three different judges or winning three lots of five points in the breed and one Group under four different judges. Where two Green Stars are offered, such as

Ch. Kerronmor Breda Louise and Ch. Teekos Just 'N' Time at Kerronmor. Owned by Moira Grant-Cooke. *Photo: Carol Ann Johnson.*

Ch. (RSA) Clari on Sweet Minx. Breeder/owner Lundi and Nigel Blamey.

in the Pug classes at the St Patrick's Day Championship Show in 1996, the award to the best dog or bitch entitles the winner to a Green Star, the value of which is at least equal to the Green Star awarded to the Best Opposite Sex. The winner of a Group or BIS is entitled to a Green Star equal in value to the highest value won by any dog competing in that Group or BIS. There are twenty-three shows held every year in which Pugs can be entered and receive the Green Star Award. The title Annual Champion is awarded each year to the dog or bitch in each breed who wins the greatest number of Green Star points, with a minimum of thirty points won under not less than three different judges. The result is published in full detail in the IKC Yearbook which is available at the St Patrick's Day Championship Show.

The Annual Champion in Eire from 1992 to 1994 was Ch. Hobbytoys Half Nelson son of Eng. Ch. Claybridge Call Me Cyril. He was bred by Mrs C. Knox and owned by Mrs R. Gleeson. The top bitch in 1992 was Ch. Hermony Lady Prunella, bred and owned by Mrs M.E. Watt. Mrs Moira Grant-Cooke has been having a good run of success recently, making up four Champions in the last three years. She is the owner of Ch. Sonsirae Becky at Kerronmor, the top bitch in 1993 who was bred by Mrs J. Kilpatrick. She is also the owner of the 1995 Annual Champion, Ch. Teekos Just 'N' Time at Kerronmor, another son of Eng. Ch. Claybridge Call Me Cyril, who is an English import bred by Mrs Jean Lockett from Merseyside. Just 'N' Time's daughter, Ch Kerronmor Breda Louise, bred and owned by Mrs Grant-Cooke, was the top bitch in 1994 and 1995.

SOUTH AFRICA
Because of the small number of Pugs in South Africa compared with England, America and many other countries, one tends to think that their existence in South Africa can only have begun in the second half of the 20th century. However, current

*Ch. (RSA)
Pugini Andreo of
Clari
(import UK).
Bred by Pat
Rufini (UK).
Owned by
Lundi and
Nigel Blamey.*

*Photo: Carol Ann
Johnson.*

research tells us that the earliest reference is a report in the Eastern Province Herald of Friday March 16th 1893 about the South African Kennel Club of Port Elizabeth's first show, which had been held on March 14th 1893. There were entries for Pugs and the first prize was won by Mr John Hall's dog Prince. The comment from the judge, Mr Howard Marblebeck, was: "It was a good all round dog and the only apparent fault was the curl of the tail." Mr Hall also won second prize with Nellie. The report on Nellie was: "It was rather too long in the tail and lacked the black streak down the back, which is necessary for the purpose of perfection."

At the first show in Capetown in December 1889 comment on the Pugs in the Cape Times was: "There was a fair display of Pugs. Mr W.J. Robertson's Pearl, a pretty miniature dog, and Mr C.T. Mill's Turk took equal placing." The first Pug registered was in 1891, breeder and date of birth unknown. A few shows are reported at the turn of the century and Mahoney,

owned first by A.G. Butow, then by E. Barnes and later by Major E.W. Urquhart, was the first recorded Champion. To become a Champion a dog had to have wins in three centres which were widespread and, as the method of transport was mostly by train, travelling was difficult in those days.

The Kennel Union of South Africa is the governing body for dogs and dog shows in South Africa and their records begin in 1934. So, from 1908 to 1934 very little information has yet been obtained and this is really quite a gap. However by 1948 things began to look up and Pugs were being imported from England. Masbeck Bullseye bred by Mrs B. Masland was the first Pug to be imported to South Africa after World War II and he was soon followed by Jennifer of Harloo, bred by Mrs L. Green. These two Pugs seem to be the backbone of good Pugs in South Africa. At a later date there was some denial of this, as no trace could be found of Bullseye's registration. Maybe he was imported but not registered with the KUSA. It is known that Jennifer was registered. More English Pugs were arriving in South Africa including Susan Graham-Weall's Phidgity Pugs, Greengables and more Masbecks. Mrs D Nicolau (Pugdale) was breeding and showing good Pugs, as were Major and Mrs Henwick. They were having a good run of success with their black Pugs. I remember them importing Ch. Polderhill King Kong from Mrs Church. King Kong was used at stud before leaving for South Africa and I owned his son, Rob Roy of Stravaich. They wanted to buy Rob Roy but he belonged to my husband and nothing would make him part with him.

Interest in the Transvaal grew rapidly in the 1980s and the Northern Transvaal Pug Breeders Club was formed. Mrs Eales, as first secretary, was importing Pugs from England. The prefixes Mondella, Cedarwood and Hazelbridge were joining her kennel and her Pugs were having a great influence on Pugs in South Africa.

The Kennel Union of South Africa is the governing body of dogs in that country. All breed or Group clubs affiliated to the KUSA have one Championship and two to five Open shows each year. The Breed Standard of the Pug is the same as that for the United Kingdom. There must be no physical alterations, for example, no clipping of whiskers and no 'touch-ups'. The Pug is allowed to be stacked and baited while showing. Classes that it is compulsory to hold in each breed at Championship Shows are Minor Puppy (6 to 9 months old), Puppy (9 to 12 months), Junior (12 to 18 months), Graduate (18 to 24 months) and Open (over 2 years). There are various optional classes such as Veteran (over 7 years), Champion and South

African Bred (any age). Champions are not allowed in any class other than their own. There are three winning placings in each class. Class winners, except those in the Champion Class, contest for the Challenge Certificate. The Dog CC, Champion Dog, Bitch CC and Champion Bitch all contest for Best of Breed. All BOB winners are eligible to enter in the Group Challenge where there are four placings. Best in Show is chosen from the Group winners.

Among the top shows there is the Dogmor Dog of the Year held in Johannesburg at the end of August. Entry is by invitation and is based on the dog and bitch in each breed who have won the most BOBs during the previous twelve months. The KUSA National Awards are held every two years. The dog or bitch must be a Champion or must have won BOB at the hosting show to be eligible to enter. A certificate is issued similar to that of Championship status. The winner may use 'Nat.' in front of the Pug's name to indicate National status. The Epol Junior Dog of the Year is held in Johannesburg in October. Entry is by invitation based on the most Best Puppy in Breed awards won in the previous twelve months.

Among the top winning Pugs in South Africa is Ch. (RSA) Clari on Sweet Minx, owned and bred by Lundi and Nigel Blamey. She has eighteen straight CCs. She was the Toy Breeders Association Best Opposite Sex in Show in 1992. In 1993 she was third in show at the Dogmor Dog of the Year and became Best Opposite Sex in Show. In the same year she was the KUSA National Pug. Ch. Pugini Andreo of Clari (UK import), born in October, 1993, is owned by Lundi and Nigel Blamey and bred by Pat Rufini (UK). He was shown as a puppy before leaving the United

Kingdom and eight times qualified for Crufts. He was winner of the first day Spillers Puppy Stakes at the Windsor Championship Show in July, 1994 and was Reserve in the Finals on the last day of the show. He was handled in these classes by Rebecca Naylor, a Junior Handler. In South Africa, Andreo has taken 21 CCs and 18 BOBs. He was KUSA National Pug in 1995, has won four straight Groups and had multiple Group placings. He was Best Puppy in Show at the TDBA Championship Show and second in the Toy Group at the Dogmor Dog of the Year Show in the same year. Clari Jollie Jhester, born March 1st 1995, was sired by Ch. (RSA) Pugini Andreo of Clari (UK import). He was winner of the Puppy Group at his debut show and looks to be following in his father's footsteps.

Hatherleigh Pugs are owned by Jack Hulley, although the affix was previously that of Mrs Eales. Jack is the Pug Historian and Chairman of the Northern Transvaal Pug Breeders Club and is presently showing a male fawn, Montnora William of Hatherleigh, which has Australian and English breeding. I have known Jack for many years and I know he has always been interested in the English-bred Pug. Manchu Pugs are owned by Rosemary Skorpen. She is now showing, with success, a very good-quality black male Pug, Manchu Black Paladin. The background of the Manchu Pugs contains English breeding such as Hazelbridge, the prefix of the late Miss Gretton who bred lovely Pugs for many years.

Haemstede and Betwinhard Pugs are owned by Stephan Bouwer and Roux Engelbrecht. In the early 1980s Stephan had a great deal of success showing Ch. (RSA) Jolunns Miles of Haemstede, a grandson of Ch. (UK) Spreadcombe Watson of Rydens ex Hazelbridge Toots Sweet. Miles was top winning South African Pug for three years running, taking many top honours. In 1984 Stephan visited Crufts in hopes of buying another Pug, but he had previously visited Holland and, with the help of Christina Veldhuis, he had fallen for a puppy in that country. Ch. (RSA and Ned.) Lubbert von Klawout of Haemstede arrived in South Africa as a young puppy and during his career won just about everything that was possible. His show history is said to be unequalled in South Africa.

At shows in South Africa there are two handling classes for young people, divided according to age. The Children's Handling Class is for boys and girls aged eight and under eleven years of age and the Junior Handling Classes is for boys and girls aged eleven to under seventeen years of age. These classes are judged on the ability of the handler to control, set up and move their dog, together with the dress and demeanour of the handler. The quality of the dog is not taken into consideration. Young people may qualify for entry into the Children's and the Junior Handler of the Year Competition.

EUROPE

Although the Breed Standard of the Pug in Europe is the same as the English and world-wide Standard, rules of individual countries regarding awards, dog shows and dogs becoming Champions do vary. However, most of them in Europe are controlled by the Rules and Regulations of International Championship approved by the Fédération Cynologique Internationale (FCI). The Kennel Clubs of Austria, Belgium, Denmark, Finland, France,

Holland, Hungary, Italy, Luxembourg, Monaco, Norway, Portugal, Spain, Sweden and Switzerland are all affiliated to the FCI. Under FCI rules the Pug is in the Toy or 'Companion' Group.

The Certificat d'Aptitude au Championnat (CAC) is awarded to all breeds of dog at certain Shows and counts towards the title of Champion in the home countries. The CACIB is the Certificat d'Aptitude au Championnat International de Beauté. This means that a dog or bitch can win a ticket (certificate) towards being an International Champion. To qualify for the title International Beauty Champion a dog must have received four CACIBs in three different countries, given by three different judges, whatever the number of competitors. One of these four CACIBs must have been obtained in the country of origin of the breed. For the Pug this would have to be China. This not being possible, the country that makes up the Standard for the breed would be accepted, which for the Pug would be the UK. This also is not possible because of quarantine regulations. So the only possibility for this CACIB in Europe would be the country where the dog lives. However, small countries, where few shows are held, may choose a neighbouring country in which this CACIB may be obtained. There are quite a number of shows where CACIBs can be awarded. The title of European Champion can be awarded at the European Show where a CAC ticket of the country who is the host of the show and a CACIB ticket for International Champion are awarded. The European show was held in Maastricht in Holland in 1995 and in Luxembourg in 1996. The World Championship Show moves to a different country every year. In 1996 the venue was Vienna. When it is held in Europe, a dog can be awarded the title of World Champion and win a CAC ticket of the host country and a CACIB ticket for the International Champion title.

BELGIUM
In 1976 there were no breeders of Pugs in Belgium recognised by the FCI and breeding with the internationally recognised Pedigree of the Société Royale Saint Hubert (LOSH). There were only a few dealers who occasionally had Pugs for sale. At this time Ingrid and Jan Mylemans decided to breed Pugs. They visited the UK and, with recommendation from Pauline Thorp, they obtained their foundation bitch, Loynerise Lively Lass, from Di Middleton. Other imports came from Jean Pearce (Pillette), Les and Elizabeth Elbourn (Bournle), Eleanor English (Rosecoppice), Nancy Tarbitt (Nanchyl) and Theo Greenhill-Reid (Ardglass). With these imported Pugs the Dylville Pugs became established and from them more kennels were started in Europe.

Both Mr Van de Weghe (Luckways Pugs) and Mrs Kissler Weidmann in Germany (Montanus Pugs) started with Dylville Pugs. Mrs Tilkin (T'Ien Tseu Pugs) started with a Pug she obtained from Mme Mortal in France and Dylville Funny Girl. I know that Mme Mortal had in the past imported Pugs from England. Miss Chapman started her Zandylane kennels with Dylville breeding and had great success. About the same time Mrs Van Pyvelde mated a Rosecoppice Sohrab (UK import) daughter to Ch. Sheafdon Peter Piper (UK import) owned by Maggie Pardaens. So this litter was nearly all English breeding. A daughter from this litter, Montanus Europa Emily, when mated to Blackseldom Wilson (UK import) produced two very nice litters.

Ardglass Tam O'Shanter with his daughter, Speedy. Best Brace in Show, Int. Ch. Show, 1995. Owned by Jan and Ingrid Mylemans and handled by their granddaughter, Kelly.

A painting of Rosecoppice Sohrab. Bred by Eleanor English (UK). Owned by Jan and Ingrid Mylemans.

Emily also had a lovely black litter when mated to Ardglass Tam O'Shanter (UK import). In 1995 Mrs Van Pyvelde visited England and purchased Sheffawn Soldier Boy to add to her Blackbirds Field kennels.

Maggie Pardaens and Mr Les Kelsbie started breeding in the 1970s with two of Mrs Young's Ryden's puppies, one black and one fawn. Later she obtained Ch. Sheafdon Peter Piper from Miss Haggie. He grew to be a handsome black dog and a most useful stud to the black bitches in Europe. Maggie has continued with her stud dogs and still has a son of Peter Piper. Her latest import is Sensayuma Jeremy. In

the late 1970s, when Ingrid and Jan Mylemans stared to breed Pugs, they decided to form the Belgian Pug Dog Club, which met with great success. With Ingrid Mylemans as their president and Maggie Pardaens as their secretary, the club has become well established, with members producing good stock. I am sure that all these English imports have been most useful to the many Pugs now being shown in Belgium and other parts of Europe. It is interesting to note that in Belgium all dogs born in 1996 had to have names beginning with U. The names of those born in 1995 had to begin with T and in 1994 it was S and so on. A dog or bitch has to be at least fifteen months old to be entered in the Open Class at a show. The Certificat d'Aptitude au Championnat (CAC) is only awarded in the Open Class and Champion Class. This means that a dog or bitch cannot win a CAC before the age of fifteen months. To become a Champion in Belgium three CACs have to be won under at least two different judges. One of the three CACs has to be won at the Brussels Championship Show or at the Club Show of the Breed Club. For Pugs this Club show is the Belgian Pug Dog Club Show. There have to be at least fifty entries at this Club show in the Open Class, Junior Class and Champion Class. Entries in the Puppy Class and the Veteran Class do not count towards the fifty entries. There also has to be at least a year between winning the first CAC and winning the last. This means that if a dog or bitch is lucky, he or she can become a Belgian Champion at the age of 27 months.

HOLLAND

The English are grateful to Holland for the Pug dog. As has already been mentioned in an earlier chapter of this book, it was the Dutch Royal family who brought Pugs to England. Today in Holland as in other parts of the world, the Pug is exhibited at dog shows and there are many breeders. The Pug Dog Club in Holland is known as "Commedia". They hold a 'members only' show where no Certificates are given. The Breed Championship show is held every two years for Pugs and it is usually judged by a foreign judge. Here a Pug can be awarded a CAC towards a Dutch Championship which counts double. The Reserve CAC is counted as one CAC instead of needing four Res. CACs to be

equal to one CAC as normal. On entering a show all breeds of dog are checked by a vet. A dog must have two testicles and the bitches are not allowed to be in season. There is also a check on the dog's papers. All dogs must be vaccinated against diseases and, of course, must have a pedigree. In Europe Pugs are groomed to keep them in the best condition. They are bathed, their noses are made shiny, toenails are cut, ears are cleaned and, before going in the show ring some training is given, just as in England.

At a Breed Championship show the Classes are the Open Class (for dogs and bitches aged 15 months and older), the Young Dogs Class (for dogs and bitches aged 18 to 24 months), the Youth Class (for dogs and bitches aged 9 to 18 months), the Breeders Class (for dogs and bitches bred by the exhibitor), the Veteran Class (for dogs and bitches over 7 years of age) and the Puppy Class (for dogs and bitches aged 6 to 9 months old). The Puppy Class does not count towards competing for the CAC.

The title Dutch Champion is awarded as soon as a Pug has won four CACs provided that the last CAC is won after the Pug has reached the age of 27 months. There are other numerous combinations with regards to numbers of CACs required for the title of Dutch Champion to be awarded. The Dutch Championship Certificate is awarded at a CAC show. Most shows are CAC shows and CACIB shows in one. The classes at one of these shows are the Open Class, the Youth Class, the Breeders Class and the Champions Class, that last class being the same as at a Breed Championship show. The Champions Class is only for a Pug who is already a Dutch Champion or an International Champion. Pugs with titles

Empereur Napoleon Pauline: 22 CAC, 12 CACIB, 19 Res. CAC, 9 Res. CACIB in 8 countries. Owner/breeder Ria Jansen.

such as Winner, European Champion or World Champion are not eligible for entry into this class. There are four placings in every class but they are not necessarily placed left to right as in the UK. Every Pug gets a written report. In the ring there is the judge, the ring steward who is in charge of the procedures in the ring and writes down the comments of the judge, and a steward for administration purposes who makes sure that everyone who has won a ticket gets one and that the handlers of the Pugs receive the written comment. A Pug who is awarded a CAC and a CACIB is given a certificat-carte on the day and then receives written confirmation of the result at home. Special prizes are often awarded at these shows. After a dog has won his class he will return together with all the other class winners for the Best Dog Challenge. The same applies to the bitches. The Best Dog and the Best Bitch are judged for BOB and then go on for the Group judging.

Pugs in Holland are called Mopshunden and it is for that reason, I am sure, that they are in the Hound Group and not in the Toy Group as in England and all the other countries that I have written about. The most important show in Holland is the Winner Show in Amsterdam which is held for two days on the first weekend in December every year. Tickets won at this show count double.

Madame Veldhuis, was a well-known breeder of Chow Chows in Holland for many years, and the fact that she had an aunt who was a Pug breeder didn't really inspire her to change breeds. However, in 1953, she went to England with an interest in the Chow Chows but she happened to come across a Pug puppy and fell for her there and then. That was the start. As we all know, once you have one Pug, you want another and so Madame Veldhuis' interest grew and grew and, up to the present day, her beautiful Pugs have won many awards and her puppies are much sought after in Europe. She has been a member of the English Pug Dog Club at least since 1957.

SWEDEN

The Swedish Kennel Club (SKK) is the governing body for dog shows in Sweden. It is responsible for all breeds and most things concerning dogs, such as registration of puppies and show results. The SKK runs the International and National Shows. The Specialklubben för Sällskaps-och Dvärghundar (SSD) is connected with the SKK and is the Special Club for Companions and Miniatures. The SSD arrange National Shows and one of them is especially for their winners. A gala called the Champion of Champions is held by the Stockholm Kennel Club, one of the many divisions of the SKK, in connection with the Easter Show. Mops Orden, the Pug Dog Club of Sweden, like all other breed clubs belonging to the SSD, must also be connected with the SKK. Small clubs like

the Mops Orden have unofficial shows where CCs are not awarded. The Mops shows often have an entry of more than one hundred Pugs. This is run on the Group system and lasts for two days. A party is held in the evening of the first day.

Official Classes at shows are the Junior Class (9 to 15 months), the Youngsters Class (15 to 24 months) and the Open Class (24 months to seven years). In each class there are three placings, given from right to left, the opposite to the UK. The judge writes a report on every dog or bitch entered and may be helped by the ring secretary to do this. This report is signed by the judge and becomes the property of the owner, who can then compare the comments with those from other judges at other shows. There are also Competition Classes at shows. In the Junior Competition Class the placings are 1st, 2nd, 3rd, 4th and Reserve. The 1st is given an Honour Prize (HP) if it is worthy. All those winning an HP go on to the Winners Class. The Youngsters Competition Class is the same. The Winners Class contains the 1st Prize Winner from the Open Class and the HPs from the Juniors and Youngsters Competition Classes. The judge awards 1st, 2nd, 3rd, 4th and Reserve with or without Certificat-equality (CK). The first with the CK gets the Certificate CC. In this way it is possible for a junior to get the certificate but a junior cannot get the CH. In the Champion Competition Class a dog or bitch can be awarded a CK. In the Veteran Competition Class (from seven years) an HP or CK may be awarded. There is also a Breeders Class, where a breeder may enter four dogs or bitches of their own breeding, and there is a Progeny Class for a sire and dam with four of their offspring. All those winning a CK may compete for Best Male

Ch. Goroda Go Go Girl (English import) with her daughter, Ch. Yrhttans Tulip and Ch. Yrhttans Rose Marine. Owned by Marianne Ekedahl, Sweden.

and Best Bitch. One of these is chosen BOB and the other becomes Best Opposite Sex. The Best Veteran is also chosen here. The BOB qualifies for the Group and the winners of all the Groups compete for BIS.

To become a Champion a dog or bitch must have three certificates from at least two different judges and must be over fifteen months old when receiving the last certificate. It is also possible for a dog or bitch to be a Nordic Champion if he or she is a Champion in any three of the Scandinavian countries, Norway, Denmark, Finland or Sweden, provided that these have been awarded by different judges. An International Champion must win four CACIBs in at least three countries and under different judges, with at least one year and one day between the first and the last. CACIBs are only awarded at International Shows.

In recent years the average number of

Pug puppies registered in Sweden has been about 157. The Breed Standard does not differ from that in England as it was originally a translation from the English. However, there are nine Groups in the SKK which differ in many ways from the UK. As in England, there is no special preparation of the Pug for the show ring other than a bath and training to stand on the table and walk steadily for the judge. Over the years Pug owners in Sweden and the other Nordic countries have been interested in introducing English bloodlines. Martlesham, Doms, Hazelbridge and Edenderry are prefixes from the past that have been behind many good Swedish Pugs and in the present day there are Bournle, Ardglass, Nanchyl and many others. Int. and Nord. Ch. Bournle Pascali (UK import), a fawn dog owned by Harriet Svensson, was the top Pug from 1985 to 1988. He was the son of Ch. Nanchyl

Xerxes. In 1989 the top Pug was Int. Swedish and Nordic Ch. Bjönhovs Bounthy Pug (ex Todomas Fancy Free, GB import). This fawn dog, owned by Ola Peterson was four times the BIS at the Mops Orden Club Show. From 1990 to 1992 the top Pug was Int. S. and N. Ch. Humlans Crawford Cream Cracker, a fawn dog owned by Kerstin Eckardt. In 1990 and 1991 his litter sister S. and N. Ch. Humlans Cheesey Cocktail Crisp was top bitch. The top bitch in 1992 was S. and N. Mumricks Madame Butterfly (by Ch. Ardglass Burlington Bertie, UK import), a fawn owned by E. Winter-Harryson. In 1994 and 1995 the top bitch was Swedish Ch. Shamrags Queen Elizabeth from a mating by Ch. Ardglass Burlington Bertie and Ch. Ardglass Irene, both English breeding. She was bred and is owned by Christina Peterson.

GERMANY AND OTHER EUROPEAN COUNTRIES

Germany has its own Pug Dog Club and a Toy Club. Puppies can be registered at both. In the early days when Pugs had no club of their own the Toy Club imported from England Cerne Mars, bred by Chris Colman. This Pug was for the benefit of Pug owners to use at stud to improve the breed. Shows and rules in Germany are according to the FCI. There are now between fifty and sixty puppies registered each year. The most important dog show in Germany is held at Dortmund. France has no Pug Dog club of its own but there is a joint club with Boston Terriers. Austria has its own Pug Dog club but Hungary does not.

THE PUG IN NORTH AMERICA

A Pug whelped outside the USA is eligible for registration in the AKC Stud Book when imported into the USA. The AKC rules allow an imported dog to be registered only if it is of a breed that is eligible for individual registration in the AKC Stud Book. The Pug which is imported must have been registered with the English Kennel Club before being exported to the USA. The pedigree of the Pug, or any other breed of dog being imported, must contain at least three generations of ancestry establishing that each dog in the three generations was of the same breed and registered in its country of birth. Each dog named in the three generations must be identified by its registration name and number. The pedigree must also include the record of transfer to the USA importer. The owner who applies to register the imported Pug must be a resident of the USA.

SHOWS

The Match show is similar to the Exemption show in England because entries are made on the day. This is a good opportunity for a beginner to gain experience as many of the procedures are the same as for a regular dog show. It is also an opportunity for a breeder to try out a litter. The age limit is reduced to two or three months at Match shows, so as to give puppies plenty of practice before they compete in a regular show.

There are two types of Point shows (Championship shows) licensed by the

Am. Ch. Dhandy's Favorite Woodchuck. Only Pug to win Best in Show at the Westminster KC Show (1981). No. 1 Pug in America in the history of the breed. Bred by Barbara Braley and Anitra Hutchinson. Owned by Robert A. Hauslohner.

Am. Ch. Wisselwood Olivia Rose: Multiple BoB and Group winner. Best Opp Sex at the Westminster KC Show 1995. From English and American breeding.
Breeder/owner Wisselwood kennels.
Photo: The Standard Image.

AKC. One is an All-breed Show which includes classes for all the recognised breeds and Groups of breeds, and the other is the Specialty show which is for one particular breed. Entries for these shows are made before the day. Classifications are listed in a schedule or 'Premium List' as it is called in America.

At a dog show in America, just as in England, the dogs in each breed are judged first, followed by the bitches. For each sex

there are six classes. The Puppy Class, like ours, is for those aged six months to one year. At the larger All-breed or Specialty shows, the puppy class may be divided into 6-9 months and 9-12 months. This is followed by the Twelve to Eighteen Month Class. The Novice Class is for dogs or bitches who have never won a first prize in a regular Class at any show, other than in the Puppy Class. Only dogs or bitches born in the USA or Canada are eligible for this Class. The Bred by Exhibitor Class is for all dogs or bitches, except Champions, that are six months or over and which are presently owned and exhibited by the same person that bred the dog according to AKC records. The American-Bred Class is for all dogs or bitches, except Champions, aged six months or over, born in the USA as the result of a mating in the USA. The Open Class is for all dogs or bitches aged six months or over whether bred in America or in a foreign country. It is usual to see the most experienced show Pugs in the Bred-by-exhibitor and Open Classes.

There are four placings in each class and each of these receives a ribbon to commemorate their win. The ribbon shows the AKC seal, the name of the show, the date and the placing. The colours are blue for first, red for second, yellow for third and white for fourth. This differs from the colours of the cards and rosettes that are awarded in England. We have red for first, blue for second, yellow for third and green for fourth or reserve.

The first prize winners of each of these classes come together in the Winners Class. From these Pugs the Winners Dog and the Reserve Winners Dog are chosen; similarly the Winners Bitch and Reserve Winners Bitch are selected. The Winners receive a purple ribbon and the Reserve Winners receive a purple and white ribbon. The Winners Dog and the Winners Bitch compete against each other and one is chosen as the Best of Winners after the Best of Breed selection. The Best of Winners receives a blue and white ribbon. Champions of either sex can be entered in the Open class, where they compete against the two Winners for Best of Breed. The BOB ribbon is purple and gold and the Best of Opposite Sex Winner has a red and white ribbon. The BOB now competes against all the other BOBs in their Group to be chosen Best in Group. There are four placings in each Group, each of which receives a rosette or ribbon of the same colour as the class ribbons. There are seven Groups in America – Sporting, Hound, Working, Terrier, Toy, Non-Sporting and Herding. The Group Winners meet in the final competition where one is chosen as Best in Show. The rosette awarded to the BIS can be red, white and blue or may incorporate the colours of the club organising the show.

The judge is always looking for the perfect Pug as he or she goes over each entry. The judge will look at the physical structure of the Pug – head, feet, bone structure, muscle tone etc. – and will take note of the dog's general condition, weight, coat condition and animation. Its gait will be observed from the front, the side and the rear. Temperament is also taken into consideration and there will be a penalty for shyness or viciousness. Judges are approved to officiate at Dog Shows by the AKC. Some are approved to judge only one breed, some judge several breeds and there are a few who are approved to judge every breed.

Although the procedure for the examination of a Pug in the show ring is

Am. Ch. Bonjor Clark Kent. National Specialty Winner. Winner of 51 Toy Groups. No. 1 Pug in America in 1983. Bred by Bonna Webb. Owned by Bonna Webb and Doug Huffman.

the same as in England, in America they do favour having professional handlers and in this way they get the best out of their Pugs. I hate to say it but English exhibitors spoil many a good Pug's chances by bad handling. I notice among the rules and regulations of the shows in America that it states "No practising allowed in the rings at any time." In the UK exhibitors are allowed to use the rings once judging is over and I have found this is a good training ground.

Many of the premium lists for American shows have classes scheduled for Obedience Trials, but Pugs in England in this category are few and far between. It is not that they cannot do it, because I have trained a Pug in Obedience myself, but I must say that this is unusual.

145

Am. Ch. Rowell's Solo Moon Rising: Winner of the Toy Group at Westminster KC Show in 1989. No. 1 Pug in America in 1989 and 1990. Dam of four Champion offspring. Breeder/owner John and Linda Rowell.

THE MAKING OF A CHAMPION

The making of a Champion in America is different from making a Champion in the UK. Firstly an American Championship is achieved on a points system. These points are awarded only to the Winners Dog and the Winners Bitch. The number of points up to a maximum of five, depends on the number of dogs or bitches your Pug has defeated that day in the classes. To become an American Champion a Pug must currently earn fifteen points. In reaching these fifteen points your Pug must have at least two major wins (3, 4 or 5 points)

under two different judges, and a third judge must also have awarded him or her points. The AKC has divided the country into zones and each year reviews the number of dogs shown in each breed within each zone. Each May the point schedule changes, based upon this review.

Perhaps the major difference between the road to becoming a Champion in America and that to becoming a Champion in Great Britain is that once an American Pug or any other breed has become a Champion then he or she no longer competes against classes of dogs or bitches other than Champions. When Champions, sometimes called Specials, are entered at shows, they compete for BOB only so that they may then compete at the Group level. It is often said that it is easier to make up a Champion in America than it is in England. I don't think one can make a comparison because the methods of making up a Champion are so different in the two countries.

In the USA the Pug Dog Club of America offers a Register of Merit (ROM) to any member's male Pug who has sired six Champion offspring or whose female Pug is the dam of three Champion offspring.

JUNIOR HANDLING

There is as great an interest in Junior Handling in America as there is in the UK. In America it is called Junior Showmanship. There are four classes in Junior Showmanship competition. The Novice Junior Class is for boys and girls who are at least ten years old and under fourteen on the day of the show and who, at the time the entries close, have not won three First Place awards with competition present in a Novice Class at a licensed or members show. The Novice Senior Class is for boys and girls who are at least fourteen years old and under eighteen on the day of the show and has the same criteria as the Novice Junior Class. The Open Junior and Open Senior Classes have the same age restrictions as their respective Novice classes. These classes are for those who have already won three First Place awards with competition present in a Novice Class at a licensed or members show. As with JHA and KCJO Handling Classes in the UK, the judging in the Junior Showmanship Competition is for handling only, not on the quality of the dog. A Junior who wins a First Place in an Open Class may qualify or may count towards qualification for entry into certain future limited Junior Showmanship Classes. Each Junior Handler has an AKC Junior Handler identification number which has to be included when entering classes.

In British Junior Handling Association handling classes, Juniors are able to handle any dog that they wish, with the permission of the owner, of course. In the Kennel Club Junior Organisation Handling Classes at Championship shows, Juniors are allowed to handle a dog or bitch registered, either solely or jointly, in the member's name or in the name of a member of the family, resident at the member's address. In KCJO Stakes Classes at Championship shows there are the same restrictions on the ownership of the dogs handled, but these classes are judged on the quality of the dog, not on handling, so they differ from the general handling classes. In America there are restrictions on dogs that a Junior can show in the Showmanship Classes. Each dog must be owned, or co-owned, by the Junior Handler or by the Junior Handler's father, mother, brother, sister, uncle, aunt, grandfather or grandmother, including step

and half relations, or by a member of the Junior Handler's household. This is where the American Junior Handler has the advantage over the British one. The dog must of course be eligible to compete in dog show or Obedience trials and must be entered in one of the breed or Obedience classes at the show or must be entered for Junior Showmanship only. In the UK dogs must be entered in a breed class to be eligible to enter in the Junior Handling class. There are also rules concerning the replacement of a dog if the Junior's dog is unable to be shown for such reasons as a bitch being in season. This does not apply in the UK.

Sitting at the ringside at Crufts 1992, I got into conversation with a young girl who was here to take part in the International Junior Handling Finals as the USA representative. Quite a tough assignment. She was then eighteen-and-a-half years old and this was her last competition because of age limit. For her test she chose to show a Pug which she borrowed from an exhibitor. All dogs being handled are borrowed dogs because UK quarantine laws do not allow them to bring their own dogs into the country. So the Juniors have very little time to get used to the dog they are to handle in the competition. When the judge made his final decision that young girl, Stephanie Lehman from California, was runner-up, in second place, after being in the ring for one-and-a-half hours. In 1993 the USA competitor was the runner-up once again when Elizabeth Schmidt took that award but this time not handling a Pug.

CHILLED SEMEN BREEDING
The United States of America is a vast country. A great deal of travelling can be

Am. Ch. Wisselwood Ebony Eyes: A black bitch with English and American breeding. bred by the Wisselwood Kennels.

involved when the owner of a bitch chooses to mate her with a dog living a considerable distance away. It is possible to send the bitch via the airlines but that can cause problems as the carrier may not accept the animal during adverse weather conditions, be it too hot or too cold. How have the Americans overcome this? These days there is the possibility of a "Federal Express" breeding: that is shipping chilled semen. This may come as a bit of a shock to us in

Great Britain but ignoring it will not make it go away. It is not a "Do-it-yourself" procedure nor a "Hit and Miss" situation. It needs careful planning and consideration and is somewhat more complex than natural mating.

Firstly there is the legal side of the matter. "The American Kennel Club will consider an application to register a litter resulting from artificial insemination of a bitch using fresh extended semen provided the semen is extracted and extended by a licensed veterinarian; the insemination of the bitch is performed by a licensed veterinarian and the litter is eligible for registration in all other respects. The semen must be extracted from males within the USA and shipped to points within the USA only." There are legal documents to be signed by the owner of the bitch, the owner of the dog and both vets involved. Then there is the actual procedure. Precise timing is essential when dealing with artificial insemination.

Some close friends, who are Pug breeders in America, told me that they decided to give it a try when a breeder from a northern state wanted to use one of their stud dogs. They said that on the appointed day, with their vet present, the semen was collected, prepared, packaged and presented to their local Federal Express office for a guaranteed 24-hour shipment. They said, "On our vet's advice, we had clearly labelled the shipping carton 'RUSH – CHILLED SEMEN,' primarily so the receiving vet's office would recognise it and its purpose. The label did, however, raise the eyebrows of the lady clerk at the express office, and she appeared visibly relieved when we explained it was for dogs." The outcome was a lovely litter of five Pug puppies. I have no doubt that at some time

*Am. Ch.
Sheffield's Little
Red Wagon. Sire
of 60 Champions.
Owned by
Margery Shriver.*

in the future we will be breeding from dogs and bitches from all over the world without the bitch having to venture further than the treatment room of the local veterinary surgeon.

THE PUG DOG CLUB OF AMERICA
In 1931 a few people decided to form a Pug Dog Club, but it was not until 1937 that they held their first show. It is the custom in America to hold shows in the same location and this, the first Pug Dog Club show, was held in with the Morris and Essex Show in Madison, New Jersey. Nothing seems to have been heard of the Club after that. The real interest in the breed appears to be around the 1950s when a few enthusiasts got together in New York City with the idea of forming a new club. The first meeting with dated minutes was December 10th, 1954 and this was the start of the Pug Dog Club of America. The names of some of the people involved are so familiar to me – Dr. James Stubbs, Mrs

Miriam Koch, Filomena Doherty and Ralph Adair. Filomena must surely have been one of the most well known and successful breeders of all times. Her Pugville kennels included many of the top winning Pugs of their day. Everyone knew of Ch. Pugville Mighty Jim, said to be the greatest Pug there was. He sired thirty-eight Champions and was awarded Best Stud Dog at five PDCA Specialty Shows. The rich and famous bought their Pugs from this lady, including the Duke and Duchess of Windsor and Princess Grace and Prince Rainier of Monaco. Especially prominent in my memory is Ralph 'Buddy' Adair who, with his wife Marion, have been close friends of mine ever since we first met in 1971. He would often ring me and his voice is still in my ears. I can hear him saying as always, in his endearing American accent, "Hello, Honey". The PDCA grew with the years and many individual clubs from other cities of the USA became members. At the present time there are 21

Am. Ch. Bonjor Peter Parker; Winner of the PDCA National Specialty 1983 and 1984. Bred by Bonna and Novual Webb. Owner/handled Alan Harper.

Pug Dog Clubs affiliated to the 'Mother Club'. In 1995 the PDCA held a very successful 40th Anniversary Specialty show. From a report I have, that was written prior to this Show, success speaks for itself.

1960s AND 1970s

During the 1960s and 1970s there were many Pugs being exported from England to America. They were very much in demand, especially blacks. The BIS at the All Breeds Show at Palm Beach, Florida, in 1960, was Int. Ch. Mirandus Invader of Harloo. He was the first black Pug to take a top honour in America. Invader was bred by Joan Greenwood of England, campaigned to his English title by Lou Green, exported by her to America and eventually owned by Mr and Mrs Hornbeck.

The American Pug at that time was getting much too big. Breeders loved the very large head and of course with the large head came the large, heavy body. However, I know that dedicated American breeders did not wear rose-coloured glasses about

Am. Ch. Martlesham Galahad of Bournle (English import). Owner/handler Richard Paisley.

Int. Ch. Mirandus Invader of Harloo (English Import). The first black Pug to take a top honour in America. BIS at the All Breeds Show, Palm Beach, Florida, 1960. Bred by Joan Greenwood. Owned by Mr And Mrs Hornbeck.

Am. Ch. Goodchance Sandetta (English import). Bred by Ellen Brown. Owner/handler Ralph 'Buddy' Adair.

this fault. I am told by English judges who have had the pleasure of judging in America in recent years that, in the years that have followed, the size of Pugs in America has much improved and so has the quality.

In the late 1960s another import from England, Dandini Boy of Doms, owned by Bill and Sue Wall, did a lot to popularise the black Pug. In the years that followed, blacks were very much in demand from English breeders, especially Hazelbridge and Rydens breeding. Joseph and Margaret Martha imported a few blacks from Mrs Young (Rydens). There are now some lovely blacks in America.

If one looks back on the pedigrees of many black and fawn American Pugs one is sure to find somewhere the prefix or affix

of many breeders from England: Swainston, Phidgity, Philwil, Hazelbridge, Edenderry, Rydens, Martlesham, Paramin, Doms, Harloo, Adoram, Bournle, Nanchyl, Gais and many others. These I hope have been of benefit to the American Pugs of today.

PRESENT-DAY BREEDERS AND PUGS

IVANWOLD
Edward and Charlotte Patterson not only breed and show top-quality Pugs but are also involved in all aspects of the Pug world. Originally established in Virginia, the Ivanwolds moved to Florida in 1974. Both Edward and Charlotte were professional handlers for many years. Charlotte judges all Toy and Non-Sporting

Ch. Charlamar's Ancient Dreamer. No. 1 Pug in America in 1984, 1985 and 1986 and the sire of 35 Champions, including Ch. Ivanwold Ancient Mariner. Bred by Mary Moxley and Charlotte Corson. Owned by Mrs Alan Robson. Handled by Charlotte Patterson.

Ch. Ivanwold Pistol Pete of Rontu. Winner of 5 All Breed Best in Show and many Specialties. Littermate to Ch. Ivanwold Senator Sam and sire of 36 Champions. Breeder/owner Edward and Charlotte Patterson.

(Utility) dogs as well as Best in Show. Edward judges Toys. From a litter of six Pug puppies born in 1976, five became Champions. One of these was Ch. Ivanwold Senator Sam, owned by Mrs R.V. Clark. He amassed fourteen All Breed BIS as well as winning the Toy Group at the Westminster KC Show in 1980. He was also twice the winner of the Pug Dog Club of America's National Specialty. Senator

Sam's litter brother, Ch. Ivanwold Pistol Pete of Rontu, won five All Breed BIS and many Specialties. He was the sire of 37 Champions and received the Mary Shipman Pickhardt award for top stud dog in 1981 and 1983.

The Pattersons campaigned the No. 1 Pug in America in 1984, 1985 and 1986, Ch. Charlamar's Ancient Dreamer, owned by Mrs Alan R. Robson. He sired 35

Ch. Ivanwold Senator Sam. No. 1 Pug in America in 1979 and 1980. Winner of Toy Group at the Westminster KC Show in 1980. 14 All Breed Best in Shows. Bred by Edward and Charlotte Patterson. Owned by Mrs R. V. Clark.

Champions, including Ch. Ivanwold Ancient Mariner. Ancient Mariner, bred by Edward and Charlotte Patterson, was also owned by Mrs Alan R. Robson and handled by the Pattersons. He was No. 1 Pug in American in 1987 and 1988 and sired six Champions. The Ivanwold Pugs that are at present being shown are continuing their breeders' successes. Ch. Ivanwold Fatal Attraction, bred and owned by the Pattersons, is a Multiple Group and Multiple Specialty winner, as is Ch. Ivanwold There You Go. The latter is producing present-day prize-winning Pugs. To date there are six Champions from this bitch.

Charlotte is the current president of the Pug Dog Club of America, a position she has held since 1991, and she served as the vice-president for the six previous years. Dr Patterson wrote the Pug column for the American Kennel Club *Gazette* for sixteen years, retiring in 1995.

CAMEO
From the Cameo kennels of Joe and Jan Ravotti some 50 Champion Pugs have been produced. In 1980 Jan bred from her first bitch, Rosened's Lotus Blossom, which was purchased from Rosemarie Knierim. Blossom was mated to Ch. Sheffield's Stuff 'N' Nonsense ROM, which produced Ch. Cameo's Orange Julius ROM and Ch. Cameo's Very Vanilla ROM (Beginners' luck, surely!). Other well-awarded Cameo Pugs have been Ch. Cameo's Cover Girl

Am. Ch. Cameo's Baby Biffle. Winner of the PDCA National Specialty Show in 1992, 1993 and 1994.
Bred by Joe and Jan Ravotti. Owned by Mrs Alan R. Robson.

and Ch. Cameo's Baby Biffle, both BIS winners owned by Mrs Alan R. Robson.

ALBELARM
Mrs Alan R. Robson of the Albelarm Kennels has been involved in dogs since childhood. She has taken top awards in Dalmatians and Pointers and has also bred and campaigned Dachshunds,

Pembrokeshire Welsh Corgis, Labradors, Shelties and Schippekes. She became interested in Pugs in the late 1970s. Her first Champion was Sheffield's Fortune Teller. Since then she has owned Ch. Charlamar's Ancient Dreamer and his son, Ch. Ivanwold Ancient Mariner. Both of these were handled by Charlotte Patterson. When Edward and Charlotte Patterson retired from handling to become judges, Mrs Robson acquired Jan and Joe Ravotti to handle her Pugs. Equal success came with Ch. Cameo's Cover Girl and Ch. Cameo's Baby Biffle, both bred by Jan and Joe Ravotti. Baby Biffle was the winner of the PDCA National Specialty Show in 1992, 1993 and 1994. She is the only bitch ever to accomplish this feat and only the second Pug ever to win the National three times. Many Albelarm Pugs have become Champions and there are always new ones waiting their turn in the show ring.

KESANDER
Jean Anderson's interest in Pugs started in 1964 with a pet fawn bitch which won her heart. Her Pug family increased and she has since had Champions in both fawn and black. Jean has favoured the blacks and has had great success with them. Her first Champion in 1974 was Kesander's Double Debbel. His son, Ch. Kesander's Speak of D'Debbel CD, ROM, became the top winning black Pug in America in 1981, 1982 and 1983 and he has passed his qualities on to his descendants. Among Jean's present-day Pugs are Ch. Kesander's Ursa Major ROM, who has sired ten black Champions, and his daughter, Ch. Moonshadow Magic of Kesander ROM, the dam of six black Champions from two litters. Offspring of these Pugs are being shown with great success at the present

time. Jean is very careful in her breeding, studying so as not to breed genetic faults.

SILVERTOWN

When Jane Lamarine's mother bought a Pug puppy, Tri-Boro's Star Chief Mate, in 1958, it opened up a new life for Jane. Chief Mate was sired by Ch. Star Jade of Northboro, owned by Mary Shipman Pickhardt, of Sabbaday fame. This chance meeting united Jane and Mary as client and handler and they became dear friends. In 1969, Polly Lamarine acquired Sabbaday Sampler, who finished her Championship at the Westminster Kennel Club Show, but she was never bred from. In 1971 Sabbaday Favor joined the Lamarines and became their foundation bitch. She gained her American and Canadian titles and became the dam of four Champions. National Specialty Show winner Ch. Sabbaday Kidd's Capricorn was owned by the famous movie star, Sylvia Sidney. Jane and Polly Lamarine have had numerous successes with their Silvertown and Sabbaday Pugs. They consider their greatest show Pug, who retired in 1996, was Am. Can. Ch. Silvertown Busy Bee. She was a stud fee puppy and a good one. As a junior puppy at the PDCA National, she won her class of 27 puppies under Les Elbourn from England. During her career she collected over 300 Best of Breed, 29 Groups, 208 Group placements, one Best in Show (Canada) and 3 Bests in Specialty show. She was No. 2 Pug Bitch in America in 1994 and No. 1 Bitch in 1995. At the time of writing, Busy Bee is still to be seen at shows taking awards in the Veteran Classes.

Am. Can. Ch. Silvertown Busy Bee. Winner of 300 Best of Breeds, 1 Best in Show and 3 Best in Specialty Show. No. 2 Pug Bitch in America in 1994 and No. 1 Bitch in 1995. Breeder Michael Fosella. Owner/handler Polly Lamarine.

BLAQUE

Blanche Roberts has owned and bred Pugs since 1969. She started with a pet Pug her mother sent to her from Boston. Attending dog shows, Blanche soon discovered what a show Pug should look like. From Paulaine Pugs she obtained a show Pug, Ch. Blaque Shahanshah of Paulaine, and made him one of the top ten Pugs in the USA for two years. Her interest grew and a show bitch

ABOVE: Am Ch. Broughcastl Balladeer. Holder of the record of the most Specialty wins in America. Twice BoB at the Westminster KC Show. Balladeer is the sire of litter mates of Ch. Ivanwold Pistol Pete of Rontu and Ch. Ivanwold Senator Sam. Bred by Jeff Webb and Doug Huffman. Owned by Doug Huffman.

TOP RIGHT Am. Ch. Broughcastl Blaque Bumblbee. Winner of 10 Toy Groups. Best Opposite Sex at the PDCA Specialty Show. In the top ten Pugs in America in 1995. Bred by W.M and Barbara Crockett. Owner/handler Doug Huffman.

ABOVE: Am. Ch. Broughcastl Blaque Bombaway. All Breed Best in Show Winner. Winner of 28 Groups. Bred by Blanche Roberts and Doug. Huffman. Owner/handler Doug Huffman.

BELOW: Ch. Fahey's Great Ball of Fire and Ch. Fahey's Fancy Pants. All Breed Best in Show litter mates. Bred by Jane Fahey.

BEST OF BREED
PETRULIS

was obtained for breeding. Since then Blanche has never looked back. She has bred 63 Champions, all attaining top awards. Ch. Bornfree Phire Fox was her single most important purchase. He sired fifty Champions. Both Phire Fox and Ch. Blaque's Streekin Deacon can be found in the pedigrees of Blaque Pugs. One of Blanche's favourites was Ch. Blaque's Artful Abbess, a small bitch of great character. When Abbess, a daughter of Deacon, was mated to Phire Fox, she produced four Champions in one litter. Recently Doug Huffman (Broughcastl Pugs) has had great success in breeding, using Blaque Pugs, including Ch. Broughcastl Blaque Bombaway, an All Breed Best in Show winner and winner of 28 Groups. Apart from breeding and showing Pugs, Blanche is an AKC judge and also has great interest in the running of clubs. She is currently vice-president of the PDCA as well as of other clubs.

WISSELWOOD

The Wisselwood Pugs, I am sure, need no introduction from me. Having had Pugs since 1964 and being a member of the English Pug Dog Club for over twenty years, Lorene Vickers-Smith and her Pugs are more than familiar on both sides of the Atlantic. Her Pugs were founded on English stock. Lorene was a great friend of Dick Paisley, whom older Pug breeders remember so well. After his fatal accident, a number of English imported Pugs, including Ch. Tick Tock of LeTasyll, Ch. Martlesham Galahad of Bournle and Ch. Phidgity Phircone, which Dick owned and campaigned so successfully, went to live with and be cared for by Lorene. Ch. Phidgity Phircone, English-bred by Susan Graham-Weall, was the foundation line of

Am. Ch. Wisselwood Bear Kat.
Bred by the Wisselwood Kennels of Terry J.
Smith, Lorene M. Vickers-Smith and Nancy
McCorkle.

Lorene's fawn Pugs and produced many Champions. His granddaughters, mated to Ch. Neubraa Papageno, English import bred by Miss Sybil Nehring, were most successful. Ch. Tick Tock of LeTasyll, another English import, bred by Mrs Nash, produced a granddaughter, Ch. Wisselwood Velvet Tubby, who was the basis for the Wisselwood line-bred blacks. Lorene is helped in the running of her kennels by her husband, Terry Smith, and their partner since 1990, Nancy McCorkle, who lives in another State. This enables Lorene to give such a lot of time in other aspects of the Pug world. She has been a member of the Pug Dog Club of America since the 1970s, where she is a past and current director and where she serves on the PDCA Ethics committee. She chairs the Illustrated Standard Committee in the

Am. Ch. Wisselwood Rasheeda Moore. A black winning bitch,
bred by the Wisselwood kennels.

HARPER

Like most of us, Alan Harper's interest in the Pug began with a family pet. By 1970 the Harper Pugs were established in serious breeding and started off in attending match shows. The more he learned about the breed, the higher were his ambitions and eventually through breeding and handling both blacks and fawns, he achieved his aim. Ch. Harper's Fawn C Pants produced two Champions, Ch. Harper's Funny Girl and Ch. Harper's Fawn Nest Flower, who continued the good line of breeding, producing Ch. Harper's Star Sapphire ROM. Star Sapphire was Best Opposite Sex at the 1979 PDCA National Specialty. Ch. Harper's Tommy Tune fulfilled great ambitions, for he became a top producing stud dog. His wonderful temperament, great qualities and perfect showmanship gained him numerous awards. Alan has studied the breed and is wise enough to use outcross sires on his bitches where necessary and still manages to keep the Harper stamp on his Pugs. Alan is an American KC judge and, apart from his own country, he has officiated in England, Finland, the Netherlands and Japan. Alan's mother, Norma, is his perfect help and cares for the kennels while he is showing and judging.

WESTON

Mrs Curtin (Betty) Weston is more than grateful that her mother presented a Pug puppy to her two children for Christmas 1961. Since that first encounter with the breed, she has owned 34 Champions, twelve of which were bred in England. Betty considers that the biggest influence of any English Pug she has owned was Am. Can. Ch. Gais Tipkins, bred by Mrs Mary LeGallais. He was born in 1975 and his

PDCA and also the American Brusels Griffon Association. She is a well-known judge both in America and in other countries. She extends her interest to Pug rescue and enjoys conducting seminars, thus enlightening the public and judges as to the true Standard of the Pug. Wisselwood currently has the No. 2 Pug and top bitch in the USA, namely Ch. Wisselwood Olivia Rose. She has had multiple BOBs and Group wins and was Best Opposite Sex at the Westminster KC Show in 1995.

qualities can still be seen in his offspring today. He sired eighteen American and five Canadian Champions. The proudest and biggest thrill that Betty has ever had in Pugs was in Chicago, Illinois, on April 15th 1978 when English judge Elizabeth Elbourn gave Tipkins Winners Dog, which finished his Championship title, and then made him BOB over twenty Champions at the Great Lakes Pug Club Specialty Show. Am. Can. Ch. Gais Jeremy Fisher sired four Champions and Gais Rufty Tufty sired nine Champions. Both these dogs have been awarded the ROM and have proved themselves good stud dogs used by many of the top breeders in the USA. Other Pugs imported from England by Betty include Brandy of Rydens, bred by Nancy Young (Rydens), who produced eight Champions, and Ch. Cerne Shamus, bred by Chris Coleman, who produced five Champions. Betty also owned Pugs bred by Joe Braddon (Ide), Miss Haggie (Sheafdon) and Miss Stinson (Baymeadows). The Weston kennels certainly must have held more English-bred Pugs than any other in the USA. Betty has lots of wonderful memories and is proud of the influence that her English-bred Pugs have made on Pugs in America.

Am. Ch. Larimar's Chip Off the Old Block, Number One Pug in America in 1991. Winner of the 1991 PDCA National Specialty and Best of Breed at Westmiunster in 1993. Owned and bred by Hazel Martens.

ROWELL

John and Linda Rowell purchased their first Pug in 1972. Their first to gain Championship status was Ch. Terytam Taskmaster in 1978 and their first homebred Champion was Ch. Rowell's Mad Bad Leroy Brown. John and Linda's success continues and to date they have bred or owned 27 Champions. They breed mainly for their own pleasure and for the improvement of the breed – not simply to sell puppies! In other words, for quality not quantity. Among their successes have been three All-Breed BIS winners, two Westminster Breed winners, one Westminster Group winner and one Westminster Award of Merit winner. They have bred or owned six multi-Group winners, five Specialty BIS winners, the top Pug for 1989, 1990 and 1992 and top ten Pugs for 1987 and 1988. What a wonderful record! Linda says that Ch. Rowell's Solo Moon Rising ROM made all her dreams come true. She was all-time top-winning

Am Ch. Larimar's Talk of the Town. No. 1 Pug in America in 1994 and 1995. BoB at the Westminster KC Show in 1995. Breeder/owner Hazel N. Martens.

bitch in breed history, all-time top-winning breed/owner/handler Pug in breed history and her numerous awards include 169 BOB. Solo had two litters of puppies, producing four Champions. Both Ch. Rowell's Cadillac Style and Ch. Rowell's Martinique are following in their dam's footsteps and are taking top awards at the present time.

SUMMARY

What a grand job the pioneers and the present committee of the PDCA have done and are still doing! What lovely Pugs are being produced in America. I do hope that the photographs I have gathered together for this book will prove what I am saying. This collection represents one of the most comprehensive group of winners and great Pugs from America ever gathered.

Unfortunately I am not a traveller so I have never had the privilege of visiting the US to see for myself, but over the many years I have been with the breed, I have been familiar with American Pugs and their breeders. Being a member of the Maryland Club for well over twenty years has kept me in touch with all events and has given me the loyal friendship of those I have known and met in the past, such as 'Buddy' and Marion Adair, Joseph and Margaret

Martha, James Cavallaro, Dr Reinitz, Charlotte and Edward Patterson and many others, some no longer with us, and we have all been linked together with one interest. A prominent American breeder, before visiting England, once wrote "possibly because many of our pedigrees list English Pugs, and because we think of England as the home of the modern-day Pug, it is assumed that the English Pug is superior overall." However, following the visit, this breeder perceived "no differences between the Pugs of our two countries – or between the breeders. We all share the same concerns, have the same problems, and love our Pugs with equal fervour. The English are as interested in the American Pugs as the Americans are in the English ones." How strongly I agree! I well remember what a thrill it was for Pug breeders in America when Ch. Dhandy's Favorite Woodchuck took top honours at the Westminster Kennel Club Show in 1981. You may not realise it but we felt the same joy here in England. Then, so many of you visited us in England to join in the celebrations at our Pug Dog Club's Centenary Show in 1983 – and what a lovely time we had! Yes, we may be miles apart but we are very close when it comes to our dear Pugs.